Say No

Stand Up for Yourself Without Looking

(Stop People Pleasing, Staying Silent, & Feeling Guilty and Unapologetically Being Yourself)

David Prince

Published By **Simon Dough**

David Prince

*Say No: Stand Up for Yourself Without Looking
(Stop People Pleasing, Staying Silent, & Feeling
Guilty and Unapologetically Being Yourself)*

ISBN 978-0-9952447-7-1

No part of this guidebook shall be reproduced in any form without permission in writing from the publisher except in the case of brief quotations embodied in critical articles or reviews.

Legal & Disclaimer

The information contained in this book is not designed to replace or take the place of any form of medicine or professional medical advice. The information in this book has been provided for educational & entertainment purposes only.

The information contained in this book has been compiled from sources deemed reliable, and it is accurate to the best of the Author's knowledge; however, the Author cannot guarantee its accuracy and validity and cannot be held liable for any errors or omissions. Changes are periodically made to this book. You must consult your doctor or get professional medical advice before using any of the suggested remedies, techniques, or information in this book.

Upon using the information contained in this book, you agree to hold harmless the Author from and against any damages, costs, and expenses, including any legal fees potentially resulting from the application of any of the information provided by this guide. This disclaimer applies to any damages or injury caused by the use and application, whether directly or indirectly, of any advice or information presented, whether for breach of contract, tort, negligence, personal injury, criminal intent, or under any other cause of action.

You agree to accept all risks of using the information presented inside this book. You need to consult a professional medical practitioner in order to ensure you are both able and healthy enough to participate in this program.

Table Of Contents

Chapter 1: Learning To Say No 1

Chapter 2: Personal Development Through Positive Self-Motivation 35

Chapter 3: Optimism Is Good For You 79

Chapter 4: Confident With An Unmistakable Vision 111

Chapter 5: Why Should I Change And Where Do I Start? 141

Chapter 6: Understanding The Importance Of Saying "No" 159

Chapter 7: Identifying Your Needs And Priorities 164

Chapter 8: Overcoming The Fear Of Saying "No" 167

Chapter 9: Saying "No" With Confidence 171

Chapter 10: Navigating Guilt And Disappointing Others 174

Chapter 11: Setting Boundaries And Maintaining Them................................. 178

Chapter 12: The Power Of Saying "Yes" To Yourself... 182

Chapter 1: Learning To Say No

Check out your place of job. You will discover pioneers who are harried, rushed, targeted, overworked, indignant, disillusioned, and copied out. Inability to delegate and trying to attend to unsolvable problems are of the exceptional wellsprings of these problems. Also, studying to u . S . A . NO in a quiet, unique, and appropriate manner is one of the first steps in having the choice to rent.

1.We do now not u . S . A . No for such a great sort of reasons:

2.We want to be loved

three.We have no don't forget inside the distinct individual's capacity to carry out the duty

4.We need to state yes due to the truth we want to HELP

5.We do not have the foggiest concept a manner to kingdom no in the right way

6.We have fallen into an instance of misshaped thinking, so we expect announcing no isn't always proper

7.We have constructed up a addiction of saying sure

eight.We do now not see a way to rent

nine.We anticipate preserving others responsible is a terrible aspect

10.You fill on your particular motive

Learn a manner to kingdom no:

Saying no need to be practiced, in particular if you have practiced being an entryway tangle for quite a while. Ouch! Was that excessively unforgiving? I needed to make certain you were perusing. If you aren't used to bringing up no it'll feel outsider, strange, and uncomfortable. Start little and easy. Practice getting wonderful at small nos. Like no to the server after they inquire as to whether or no longer you want a beverage other than water on the café.

Or however no in your teenager when they have spent their remittance. Or but no to the night time accumulating wherein the list of people to wait accommodates of any such massive type of folks that rub you the wrong way. What's greater, at art work exercising disapproving of these that you do now not deal with at any rate on the start.

Your diploma of passion, or absence of it, is important in having the selection to united states of america no correctly.

What is the excellent viable stage of feeling or passion? Take a stab at saying no with a similar level of love that you may make use of while you ask, "Please pass the salt?"

Timing is essential too. Sometimes a wonderful is more cushty and quicker. Remember that expression high-quality becomes a dependancy. Like a few special conduct, the extra you u . S . Yes, the more tough it is going to be to u . S . A . No.

Four Different Ways to state no:

1.No.

Sometimes sincere is ideal. No is a beautifully turning into response to an inquiry, for instance,

"Joe, I am so overworked, and you've got finished your errand at the mission. Might you be capable of pitch in and help me whole mine?"

"No"(masses of the time what the person is saying interior is: "I am getting paid a comparable reimbursement as you and will collect a comparable early consummation praise as you. However, I become too bustling buying at the net to finish my art work. What's extra, I want to pc virus out in advance of time table for the ball endeavor, and you are the sort of sap you always usa sure. Would you be capable of pitch in and help me whole my project?")

There-did no longer that make it less complex to us of a? "No."

2.Since a vast lot of you could discover this excessively complicated, and it feels crude in case you do no longer have an extraordinary affiliation with the other character, how about we strive a extraordinary way-

"I'd want to. I can not hit do what you are soliciting for that I do thru the Tuesday afternoon due to date you've got got asked. Now, I may additionally possibly do this for you with the resource of next Thursday, and I may want to ensure that it would be finished through the Thursday after that. Is that correct sufficient? No, very an lousy lot we have to stroll over and take a look at whether Suzy have to assist you?"

How became that? Practice, exercising, and additional exercise.

Now, the following one is fairly harder. What range of you want to disapprove of your chief?

3."I'd love to Boss. I am route energized by means of way of this. Incredibly, we are taking this on. Now please display to me which one in each of your needs you need me to descend the listing so I can wholesome this in so I apprehend the way to put together. Is this venture increasingly more vital or masses a good deal less vital than challenge J? Is this challenge extra critical or tons less vital than task Z? What's extra, which extra assets are to be had to art work on this mission? If none, which assets could likely you want me to take from exquisite undertakings?"

Lastly:

four. "Chief, I am so began up that we're at prolonged very last taking a have a look at this. I concur with you in this project being remarkably proficient. I aid the way you regarded into capacity options. I am in finished association with you at the assets much like the employer. I think the time-define for fruition is proper on course moreover.

I might probable need to attempt a notably one in all a type method. I'd which encompass you to guide me in hard x in choice to y for the subsequent one hundred twenty days. We will location a stake in the sand at 100 twenty days. If you and I are not content material fabric fabric with typically settled upon measurements at the multi-day marker, at that factor, I will hammer the brakes on and run corporation at Y. Would you be able to help me in that?

Comprehend that version #four above need to be utilized if you have a file of truthfulness in conjunction with your leader. This isn't always something a good way to paintings in case you are sparkling out of the sphere new in your function.

Why?

Because your supervisor may not have the incentive to help you, what's greater, primary beneath likewise need to be applied if you have a record of truthfulness collectively along with your leader.

Why?

Because severa managers have to be given as actual with that you would sand sack the challenge with the intention that you may attempt your answer.

For more credit score score score exercising the use of approach 4 from above in four precise techniques.

1.You can't assist contradicting chief and assist them via obliging their desire

2.You can not help contradicting leader and request that they assist you for your picked manner

three.You concur with subordinate and manual them via obliging their desire

four.You can not help contradicting subordinate and request that they oblige your choice

Learn to disapprove of weights that don't have a place in your shoulders. At this degree, you will have the hazard to express sure to playing in the downpour at the side of your youngsters. You can also additionally have the chance to unique positive to inspecting Spanish earlier than your get- away to Belize. You will possibly say tremendous to maintaining your mate's hand and taking a walk after supper.

Intelligent Optimism

Scientists have, as of late placed that piece of the optimism we enjoy is pressured-in. It is genetic. This isn't always particularly terrific, as a huge portion of our attributes is genetic. Besides, it's miles easy to look that a few human beings are hundreds greater positive and thrilled than others. It appears to move lower back typically to them, and this is no uncertainty because of the reality they have got hundreds steadily inherent (genetic) optimism. In any case, this can be an difficulty for some. Because of this careworn out-in thing, scientists have found that numerous people have unrealistically excessive requirements. They choice to be extra powerful than they become being, they desire to stay longer than they do, and that they choice to be greater cushty than they may be - with out placing tons exertion into it.

Does this mean we should be cautious approximately being excessively positive? Unquestionably no longer, but regardless we ought to be cautious. We, as a whole, recognise that optimism is a honestly best feature, and that superb people benefit from more than one factors of view. They have better properly being, stay longer, and make extra money than cynical human beings. Thus, paying little thoughts to how optimism is acquired, it's far as yet crucial to domesticate and make bigger it. Furthermore, regardless of whether or now not or no longer you do now not have pretty some wired-in optimism, you can, in any case, determine out the manner to be a really constructive man or woman. Everything essential is the ideal method and workout.

What is optimism?

I'm positive that everybody has a actually real concept of what optimism is. The phrase reference definition is "the choice that the proper final consequences will display up." It's related to accept as true with. However, it's no longer the identical. On account of expectation, there may be a part of self assure; you're wishing for some thing and characteristic "self assure" it's going to happen. Optimism is, glaringly, likewise associated with the selection for a incredible very last consequences, yet we are confident a few element will show up due to the reality we take into account in ourselves. We apprehend we have had been given the stuff to perform it.

How about we skip now to what optimism need to not be. As a be counted quantity of first significance, it should no longer be unrealistic. Wishing for a few thing you genuinely recognize you may in no manner get does no longer make an entire lot of revel in. (Obviously, it's far continuously important to undergo in mind that surprising matters can be accomplished with sufficient tirelessness and guarantee.)

Reasonable optimism likewise isn't the view that "the whole lot is tremendous" and the whole lot will generally come up ruddy. This is commonly referred to as complete optimism, and it is a few factor you want to be cautious about. Try now not to be idealistic to such an quantity that you're assured not anything terrible will ever display up. If you do, you might be in for a stun when it takes region. Life is brimming with troubles, and also you have to no longer dismiss them. You must confront them head-on, and live on or acclimate to them, and constantly remind your self that each one troubles have arrangements; it's far genuinely a query of locating them.

Intelligent Optimism

Along those traces, entire, unrealistic, optimism isn't what you want to cultivate and amplify. What you surely want is "clever optimism," and as we can see, the way to it is knowing. For clever optimism, a practical mind-set is needed. Furthermore, this indicates you need to begin through figuring out topics that you can not trade and awareness on what you could exchange or beautify. Besides, you need to be confident that irrespective of whether or not or now not or now not some issue unlucky takes area, you may renowned it and parent out a way to transport beyond it.

Intelligent optimism is a capacity, and prefer any information, it very well may be scholarly. Also, as exceptional talents, it requires a method of "experimentation." Try some component - deliver it your the entirety - except if it does not artwork, have a skip at a few element awesome.

At remaining, it's miles crucial not actually to make use of the presence of mind and notion, yet to likewise use your innovative thoughts. Envision the final outcomes of what you choice for - consider it powerful. Envision the prizes you may get, and the way you may experience. Play this time and again in your thoughts. Concentrate on it. This will gasoline your optimism.

Qualities of People with Intelligent Optimism

They have a realistic mind-set in the course of life. They realize that lousy matters can take place. However, they will be confident they may be able to flow past them.

They are excited about their future, however now not unrealistic.

They arise toward the beginning of the day with the sensation that the day beforehand could be a standout among others they have got ever expert.

They well known matters - understand that it is probably hard to exchange amazing topics, but they do no longer give up efficiently.

They employ their expertise to encourage optimism.

They don't forget misfortune to be transitory, and as some thing that may be survived.

They consider in what they're doing.

They take transport of that their private exquisite is however to return back decrease back.

They seem upbeat and thrilled greater frequently than not.

They renowned what they've.

Procedures for Acquiring Intelligent Optimism

1.Keep in mind what you absolutely need is smart optimism - no longer unrealistic optimism. But, keep in mind your capacities and strengths.

2.Focus for your strengths, no longer your shortcomings.

three.Try now not to pressure over what you can not trade. Focus on things you could exchange.

4.Gain out of your mishaps and mistakes.

five.I want to achieve success.

Revelation of Optimization Practices

This week, we would really like to talk about the trouble of optimization simply as a part of the do's and don'ts at the same time as enhancing. The below practices allude to upgrading computerized searching for and selling techniques with a focus on foreign exchange. While the underneath strategies may be related to any mechanized system, the foreign exchange marketplace and MetaTrader four is applied in the majority of our examples.

In rundown, optimization can be characterized as a device that therefore well-knownshows the most profitable contributions for a foreign exchange robotic. For example, foreign exchange robots can also furthermore have man or woman count on income and prevent-loss parameters (for instance, TP = 50 and SL = 15). Utilizing the MetaTrader 4 platform, those parameters may be optimized to locate which values for assume income and stop Loss should go back the maximum benefit.

When walking an optimization, it's miles important to don't forget that the top settings positioned with the resource of optimization are not usually the brilliant settings. Consider it, if you run an optimization of taking income, prevent loss, and shifting conventional incentive for all of 2009, the settings you locate are the excellent settings for 2009! Markets are typically showing signs and symptoms of alternate and due to the truth you've got the top settings for consistent with week in the beyond, a month inside the past, or a three hundred and sixty five days inside the past, does no longer imply they will maintain on appearing admirably on live market data. What is optimization great for at that point? Great query!

Optimization is a wonderful starting stage to find a few settings which have labored nicely formerly and can maintain on going for walks admirably in a while. For instance, we need to recall we ran an optimization of assuming profits and forestall loss for 2009, and the top settings ended up being TP = one hundred and SL = 50. Since we recognize what the top settings were for 2009, how approximately we comply with those settings to three marketplace statistics outside of 2009; we have to then run a easy backtest the use of those settings on market records from 2008. This is gotten once more to an out of sample test due to the truth the records you're utilizing the method to is out of doors of the optimization pattern. If you directed a totally very last take a look at inner 2009, it might be an brilliant backtest due to the reality that is the period the technique turned into optimized on.

After we find our top pattern for 2009 and apply it to out of pattern market information (2008), we're capable of make higher choices approximately our technique. If the anticipate profits and stop loss of a hundred and 50 artwork wonders in 2008, awesome, we should without a doubt have a few element here! This discloses to us that even in a unmarried-of-a-type market situations, those parameter values held up; actually encouraging locate! Then again, if the technique bites the dirt even as you operate it on virtually one in every of a kind marketplace records, that need to display screen to you the settings you're making use of maximum possibly might not keep up. Now, you will return to the true 2009 optimization, find out any other pair of parameters that labored properly, and supply them a shot 2008 (or any out of pattern facts). The manner may be complicated, but optimization serves as an outstanding tool for customers who knowledge to make use of it. Below we are going to deal with extra subjects within the realm of optimization.

Over-optimization

This term is applied reliably with "bend becoming." What happens is that on the equal time as you over-optimize settings for a selected technique (optimize right proper down to every modest element), the give up end result is a momentous backtest for the optimization time body. This guarantees splendid questioning backtest and a notable charge bend. Notwithstanding, whilst you exercising the ones parameters to a stay account, the gadget pretty regularly loses coins. You have wholesome the method to at least one set of market facts, as we talked about, that may be a fundamental no-no. You want the set of parameters that is the most sturdy and exchanges nicely on some of marketplace statistics.

Walk Forward Optimization

Walk Forward Optimization is considered as the perfect kind of optimization, and notwithstanding the reality that it is time-devouring, it places any forex robot to a definitive check. Inside walk beforehand optimization, you begin thru strolling an optimization for a specific time body, for instance, how about we take optimization for all of 2008. After the optimization is finished, to procure the most fundamental settings and lead a back test with them on data that pursue the optimization window (2008). Because we optimized for 2008, we are going to take the pinnacle parameters and run a lower decrease back take a look at for the number one 4 months of 2009 (we applied the number one four months because, for the walk-ahead test, you want to use a window one fourth the scale of the optimization window). So once you check your method at the number one four months of 2009, you can get a notion of methods your machine does on out of sample facts, fast following an optimization. If your approach does adorable, that could be a splendid beginning, the subsequent step is to stroll the machine in advance and optimize for February of 2008 to January of 2009, and in a while lead a decrease decrease back take a look at for February of 2009 to May of 2009 and verify the out of sample buying and selling. When you're accomplished, you're taking a gander at how your technique performed on the out of sample tests, if buying and selling is dependable, you may retain onward to live information testing, if it's far powerless, you should remember a wonderful robotic or probably refining how you're using the parameters.

Most likely the above machine is extended and time expending, that is why we've got got planned our strategies for optimization known as save-optimization. This method includes directing an 18-month optimization on the ultra-present day marketplace statistics (January 2009

June 2010) and in some time locating the top settings. When you have got got the principle 20-30 settings, you again take a look at them during a multi-twelve months time frame (decrease back to 2000) and test whether or not there are settings that exchange thoroughly more than ten years. If you've got a tool that transfers well in contemporary years, this is a few factor that shows terrific guarantee, and you're most possibly prepared for live demo checking out. Our methodology with hold- optimization is that the cutting-edge innovation, accumulated information, and cost movement is limited to the most contemporary marketplace information. So, having an optimization on overdue marketplace facts allows you to find the parameters which have held up in the gift, and probable from the begin (this is uncovered through the multi-12 months back check). Give it a shot; it isn't as hard because it seems.

I virtually sold a robotic, presently what?

If you have as of overdue offered a forex robot and need to test it for maximum brilliant settings, we prescribe you start via the use of taking a gander on the outdoor parameters of the robot. These are the subjects in the records area for the android, because of this if you double-faucet the robot inside the manual window and snap the facts sources tab, you could see the rundown of outer parameters. These are the matters that can be optimized; you have to recognize what they do in advance than you start an optimization. More often than no longer, the subtleties of the parameters are included into the manual for the foreign exchange robotic, and in the event that they aren't, we prescribe you touch the engineer to assist amplify on what every placing does.

Important Life Connection

I am aware about no included strong of definitive forces of the general public however the humans themselves: and at the off hazard that we count on them no longer illuminated enough to exercise their manipulate with a proper attentiveness, the cure isn't always to take it from them however to suggest their carefulness. - Thomas Jefferson

Society is composed of humans collectively with you and me. We are running gadgets of thoughts, frame, and spirit. Together, the 3-manner affiliation chooses and does our each day works. Accordingly, an combination reality is created shared via the way.

The universe is continuously displaying signs of trade, and the whole lot in the global affects the entirety else. People are not separate, however, jogging segments of an exquisite entirety. The unit is on a par with the fellowship of its man or woman. Each person holds importance in the effect of the organization.

ONE BAND, ONE SOUND: Can you envision a society wherein every person works on the right particular human limit? Envisioning this might be quite a test because it gives off a strength of being outlandish. Have you heard the expression, "To trade my disposition, you need to first of all alternate yours?"

Each succesful grown-up is at closing in fee of oneself. We have all that is anticipated to streamline our essential elements. A negligible degree of time and consideration had been given to the 3 essential parts of our lives can notably make a difference in any person. Only alternate affects the extraordinary whole, no matter whether or no longer powerful or horrific. Positive modifications in an individual will truly regulate the walking of the unit. Is it real that you are strolling searching after business?

MIND-BODY-SPIRIT CONNECTION

There is a 3-route affiliation amongst mind, frame, and spirit. Together they layout the moments of our lives. The intuitive mind works within the again of the scene manifesting planted concept and conviction seeds, whilst the cognizant mind translates and reacts to encounters. Having the right mind is further as critical as having a healthful frame and a sustained spirit.

How is your thoughts? Is it colorful or entire? Does it think properly underneath strain? Is it flexible to change? Is it that you are equipped to consider things and set up as indicated by means of way of short importance? Would you be capable of create exceptional materials for yourself and those around you? These are the whole lot the human mind is capable of.

Emotional sludge can slow intellectual capacities. Inordinate encounters of struggle or flight initiation now not simply set off development of guarded electricity that can harm an invulnerable framework, it furthermore motives past emotional reactions to sports and conditions to live dynamic and to unknowingly create contemporary-day comparative situations. When this takes region, the mind can't art work as in step with layout because of dread and moreover, anxiety.

Consider the individual inside the scenario below.

A multi-year aged person call Mildred and her husband of 25 years as of past due separated. The maximum crucial aspect she feels she want to be appreciative for is the manner that their children are currently both advanced and hitched with kids. She as soon as cherished this man. Presently she detests his guts!

Mildred is angry due to how she feels within the wake of having her ex obscenely exposed with their nearby neighbor. She discovered out the wedding would not ultimate the day they were hitched after he coincidentally known as her an beside the factor call. Presently she feels moronic for intending with the carrier and giving him her the entirety at some point of her dusk years.

Mildred's ex and father are only alike. Both talked to her like she changed into useless. Indeed, she is damaged, as indicated thru her convictions.

If she had any surely nicely worth, her husband ought to no longer have undermined her, and her dad have to have cherished her. She fizzled at nice each. These are the contemplations which is probably flowing in Mildred's heart and mind.

In the wake of sitting in the 4 dividers of her studio apartment irately thinking again about the life she as quick as lived in a five-room domestic wherein she and her ex added up their children, Mildred takes her tote from the kitchen bar, and keys from the divider established key-holder and heads to the community bar. Perhaps she'll find out another guy who will love her superior to whatever her dad and ex. She wipes away tears, locations on her undertaking face, and recognizes her lifestyles. Genuine affection proper right here she comes.

OK, united states of america Mildred's mind is strolling at immoderate best ideal working? Why or why no longer? In slight of the statistics given within the state of affairs, do you receive she will be able to find out what she is seeking out?

I'm exceptional, if we're honest with ourselves, you and I each have had moments in our lives wherein our minds labored ineffectively. Emotional sludge is simply one motive at the back of a weary spirit. It is the most effective I will supply interest to on this chapter.

There is a first-rate chemical that might clean irksome sludge and reestablish highbrow capacities. Love is an emotional sludge chemical. It is capable of placing aside obstinate discernments and convictions that hold the mind complete and crippled. It will show fact covered up under messy lies and find out why pessimism is immoderate.

The undefeated stain expelling depth of affection will easy any location of human existence that it's far associated with; thoughts, frame, and spirit. Purging emotions with love may have mental wheels turning with clever electricity. In this attitude, new capacity consequences are opened.

The human thoughts works great at the same time as practiced and enlightened. There are a greater significant wide type of techniques than I can rundown to perform this. Working riddles, math problems, and playing highbrow drawing in video games can animate and decorate intellectual making prepared. Perusing books, magazines, and using the net or published duplicate are high-quality tactics to acquaint your thoughts with illuminating records. An enlightening thoughts is one that is engaged.

Harmony is important for highbrow clarity. Contemplation, hand accessible fighting, unwinding track, and being innovative are tactics to outfit proper serenity. Fuse an movement into your lifestyles that encourages intellectual clearness. To create a spotless clean thoughts is to have a glad one!

With a colourful, completely energized mind, you may address the frame and spirit. If you resemble maximum Americans, you consider your body at any charge as quickly as every day for some reason. The hefty mindfulness has a few people fixated on their frame questioning they are excessively speedy, at the identical time as ones neglected inside the publicity take delivery of they'll be too skinny. My sister, who is five' 8", allows she is overly tall while my multi-12 months-antique little female, who is four', grumbles approximately being excessively brief.

My steerage for constructing up and preserving up a healthful frame: Eat suitable factors of right healthful nourishments, take excellent vitamins and improvements and drink masses of water. This is the excellent healthy dietweight-reduction plan for anyone type. Address your scientific medical doctor in advance than starting new systems.

I moreover suggest often walking, no matter whether or not or not just a few short get rid of in an afternoon. Your cardiovascular framework will thanks with outstanding going for walks. Make advantageous to wear supportive footwear for you to constant your lower legs and knees. Characterize focused on muscle bunches with brief fiery sports. Most importantly, deliberately envision yourself displaying your maximum green body kind, regularly. Act in self belief and entire conviction that you could accomplish your longing.

We have cited highbrow and body walking in the three section affiliation. For motives unknown, in this society, the territory of spirit is a sensitive undertaking for some. Having a healthful spirit is critical to talk human prosperity generally, so I locate it necessary to talk approximately on this bankruptcy. Spiritual associations have an impact on each other region of man or woman lifestyles. A high-quality spirit gives nicely-being.

You had been created with love from love with the purpose to love. It's a given; love is important to have a moderate, happy spirit. Open your coronary coronary coronary heart and thoughts at some point of each day interactions with distinctive humans. Begin to recognize the nearness of love whilst delivered; however throughout an thrilling experience at the grocery store. The recognition of love reinforces the functionality to precise love. Love lets in you to be nearby of the maker. This is the region spirit commonly feels unfastened.

When your thoughts is obvious, the body feels suitable, and spirit is happy you take care of business. Different topics won't be as you want them to be. However, you are in a situation to create with accuracy. Your needs are a realistic concept away. Deal collectively with your complete self; thoughts, body, and spirit to get underway awesome change as a manner to generally boost you to concealed statures. Your electricity vibrations will resound into the universe and reflect self. I count on which you mirror concept.

Chapter 2: Personal Development Through Positive Self-Motivation

Self-Motivation in a excessive exceptional manner is an internal energy that drives optimism out without hesitation for winning in life. Winners are pushed thru preference! A winner will need to improve upon their very very very own development. There turned into not a consistent winner in any stroll of life, who failed to want to win disguised. Winners understand that the essential behavioral axiom in lifestyles is the truth which you and I do glide within the direction of becoming our opinion of maximum. You and I are persuaded every day and moved by using the usage of our currently prevailing issues. As such, we skip without a doubt in the course of that what we harp on.

Everyone in life is self-persuaded, a piece bit or a wonderful deal, simply or contrarily, even a choice to do not anything is a choice relying on belief. Inspiration is a electricity which moves us to hobby, and it springs from inside the person. Motivation is characterized as a sturdy purpose far from or towards an item or condition, and it thoroughly can be created and observed, it does no longer want to be characteristic.

Positive Self-Motivation Puts You in The Driver's Seat of Your Life

Anybody wishing to enhance upon their private development desires to by using hook or through manner of crook touch off their motivation. For a long term, it's been wrongly predicted that motivation is extraneous, that it thoroughly can be siphoned in from the outdoor through upward push up and pass talks, or annoying situations or encourages. Such physical sports do supply thoughts in steerage, manual, and motivation for human beings to reveal on their progressive powers, but truely in the occasion that they need to and merely if disguised.

That is the thriller; enduring alternate is affected virtually while the need for exchange is each comprehended and disguised. Until the reward or motivator has been hindered and disguised, it has no motivational power with the useful resource of any manner. So, the actual champs in life are the people who have created, due to a famous body of mind of notable self-hope, or optimism, a robust terrific self-motivation. This is a key to enhancing your very private improvement.

At the surrender of the day they built up this ability to move within the route of dreams that they set, or jobs they want to play, and they will persevere thru nearly no diversion from moving within the route of the ones targets. In the face of all discouragement, missteps, and misfortunes, this internal force maintains them shifting upward closer to self-delight. Motivation is an emotional state, and the exquisite physical and intellectual motivators in existence, as an instance, survival, hunger, thirst, retribution, and love are altogether accused of feeling.

The key feelings which weigh down all human concept with inverse; but, almost equal results are worry and preference.

Fear is the most strong cynical helper of all; fear is the tremendous compiler and the excessive inhibitor, fear confines, fixes and frenzies, forces and at closing leaves plans and annihilations goals. Fear can pulverize someone's personal improvement and inhibit any try to improve it. Desire conversely resembles a strong fantastic magnet; reaches opens, coordinates and it draws in and energizes, and accomplishes goals.

Fear and desire are posts separated, and they result in opportunity fates in life, worry typically looks to the beyond, and desire seems to what's to come back. Fear vividly replays common reviews of failure, ache, dissatisfaction, and disagreeableness and is a hounded reminder that comparable experiences are in all likelihood going to rehash themselves. Desire as an alternative triggers a memory of pleasure and fulfillment, and it energizes the want to replay these and to make new triumphing reviews. The devouring jail phrases of the fearsome man or woman are probable going to be, I want to, I can't, I see hazard, and I desire. Be that as it could, choice says I want to, I can, I see an opportunity, and I will. Want is that passionate kingdom among wherein you're and in which you want to be. To have a achievement personal improvement, we want to determine out the manner to manipulate fear surely as with choice.

In existence, winners realize that their presently overwhelming contemplations will manage the majority in their movements and that you cannot harp at the transfer of a concept. That is why you can not get in shape if you keep thinking about how fats you'll be; you can not give up smoking in case you find out your self to be a smoker and further you cannot get wealthy if you are burdened over your bills. Winners endure in mind the chance to be an opportunity, they see the rewards of success in advance, and they do not see the punishments of failure. They feel non-public to be as a terrific step closer to a superior lifestyles. People overwhelmed with the resource of manner of dread can't act with selection or decisive aim; they enjoy life reacting in protecting.

It's an unusual and calming reality that the component we worry maximum, we feature to skip. Deep studying is the correct intellectual anecdote, for worry, and misery. Desire sparks hobby which consumes excessive adrenaline in the framework. It keeps the thoughts occupied and the expectancy of feat alive. High achievers in lifestyles have robust self-improvement capabilities, and that they maintain a high degree of concept. The struggling power that movements them to movement originates from inner their selves. Success in life is not saved for the couple of; success is reliant upon strength and backbone.

We want to have a look at and take into account how to build up this triumphing movement nature of extraordinary self-motivation. It's crucial with the intention to bear in mind that everyone is self-stimulated, both a hint bit or a excellent deal, truely or adversely and that motivation isn't discretionary, even the choice to do now not whatever is a motivation. Our fears or our dreams convince every one people. Anxiety is unavoidable due to the reality it could get you out of chance and spare your lifestyles, it is able to hold a kid's lifestyles, however as a habit or a way of life, worry has an amazingly risky response.

Fear is a crimson moderate that can prevent unstable conduct, but preference is the inexperienced moderate that releases you ahead closer to your targets. So your maximum treasured exercising in growing first rate self-motivation is to try to supplant fear motivation with preference motivation. Luckily, because of the fact worry and desire are elements of a similar coin, this is not as hard because it seems, with the resource of all payments, to be. Fear of poverty may be supplanted with a need for affluence.

Fear of suffering may be can be supplanted with a choice for correct properly-being;

dread of unhappiness may be modified with a passion for fulfillment. Every this form of actions must be gift to perform progressed personal improvement. A loss of attempt is equal to giving in; whilst there may be no real try to search for development, there may be no development the least bit to get satisfaction from over. Try not to provide the concern of failure a risk to surrender you on your adventure for greater massive non-public improvement, hold onto the desire for complete achievement and actual-existence pleasure. Winners apprehend that their presently triumphing idea spurs them, so your attention have to be on the praise of the achievement which you search for, rather than the capacity punishment of failure. Make choice your currently overwhelming idea, and it will compel you with the motivating strength for success in all factors of your each day life.

Behind each winner is a deep yearning of optimism and exuberance in the direction of the praise of achievement and now not the punishment of failure, near the association instead of the troubles and within the route of the right response as opposed to the inquiry. Behind every winner are the passionate longing, absolutely the want, and the endless strength for complete progressed personal development.

To Follow are Some Action Reminders Towards Positive Self- Motivation!

For one element, supplant the phrase can not address can inside the everyday jargon, can practice to about 90 5% of the problems you enjoy.

Next, supplant "attempt" with "will," for your every day jargon, that could be a form of semantics and builds up your new mentality of dwelling on topics you can do in place of on objects you want to try with that incorporated excuse earlier for practicable failure. Focus all your strength and interest at the fulfillment of the intention you are engaged with the prevailing second; brush aside the results of failure. Keep your force for private development at the vanguard of your thoughts.

Failure is only a transitory exchange in direction to type you out to your next achievement. Remember, you usually get what you recollect most. Next, make a rundown of your five maximum pressing desires or goals, and best alongside every, located down what the end result or advantage is whilst you accomplish it. See this rundown in advance than you head to sleep every night time and after waking each morning. Always deliver association situated input at the same time as people disclose to you their issues. When the troubles are your very personal, recognition on the fast concept..."What's the proper reaction?" Seek out and communicate with someone this week that is currently doing what it's miles you want to do maximum, and be sure that it's far someone who is doing it nicely. This applies to something, acquiring, or selling, snowboarding, or performing, talking, overseeing, or notwithstanding being an amazing associate or determine.

Find a expert, get the records, make a project of having the dangle of the whole lot you can approximately different winners inside the situation.

Enroll in a category to observe it, get personal sports activities activities, and convey fervor thru mentally searching yourself getting a price out of the achievement. At closing, make it a dependancy for each one in each of your goals, to rehash, and all all yet again, "I want to, I can, I want to, I can." The power those steps may have at the improvement of your private improvement is immeasurable. You will sense empowered, fortified, and a achievement; now not whatever can prevent you, your achievements will heap one upon every other, you'll apprehend what real personal development seems like in real life.

How To Change Your Life For The Better

Change is an inescapable thing which has an incredible sensational effect on our existence. Each new day is an possibility to alternate our lifestyles for the higher. Varieties embody us, and there's no evading change because it will discover us, challenge us, and power us to reconsider how we supply on with our existence.

Feeling down channels your power, expectation, and stress, making it hard to do what you want for a superior lifestyles. Be that as it can, you can't avoid alternate because of the reality the extra you oppose it, the more difficult your lifestyles turns into.

It has this uncanny capacity to upward thrust up to speed with you at the same time as it's far the least expected and might make an uneasy feeling or an upbeat one on your existence. At those moments, you're regarded with deciding on a desire or being pressured to do it.

Transforming your self for a advanced one isn't always a quick or easy restore. However, it's far some factor however an superb accomplishment. Unpredicted instances are likewise now not something you can wake up from. However, you can have more power than you understand.

Know the Process of Your Mind

You need to recognize that your cognizant getting ready thoughts goes at one hundred miles for each hour round your cerebrum on the equal time as your oblivious coping with is going spherical one hundred,000 miles for every hour spherical it. It is this kind of exceptional accomplishment; wouldn't it not say it isn't always?

In this manner, it means that your conscious is most effective a spectator to what your oblivious directs as it's far the best making each one of the choices in advance than you even concept of you make a decision. Regardless you do now not believe me?

An ongoing disclosure uncovers that your unconscious thoughts frequently predicts the selection or the reaction you have been going to make, as long as seven seconds earlier than your conscious mind is aware of approximately what's happening.So, at the equal time as you can take delivery of as genuine with that you have quite nowadays settled on a preference, seven seconds in advance than that, your oblivious has clearly taken a gander at all of the alternatives and made the choice you made.

What should you be able to do? The secret is to recognize that you have a time fringe of seven seconds.

Alistair Horscroft, an Australian speaker, stated for his TV affiliation "The Life Guru," has the reaction to those seven seconds and made a video about it.

Change is a Catch-22

Change resembles a Catch-22! It requires movement; but, taking movement while you are hit or damage is not easy.

Change, for the maximum detail, emerges on your existence due to a desire or an emergency, or thru way of some twist of destiny. It isn't always clean, genuinely whilst you come to discover your self at a depressing spot. It is then which you want to look the manner to regulate your factor of view to deliver you lower back up.

Since instances or issues in your life appear excluded; they thump you wobbly with a feeling of perplexity, on occasion in dread, and depart you injured, every now and then profoundly.

You can not hold a strategic distance from startling activities from taking region, control them, or understand why you're encountering such finding out moments. In any case, you can pick out out a manner to react to them. Your selections are what are empowering you to make modifications to beautify topics or now not.

What pursues are a few tips at the most talented technique to trade your lifestyles, grade by grade, to find out yourself adapting higher to unanticipated situations and occasions that emerge.

Keep Your Dreams Alive

When troubles hit us, we incline to pull once more and separate. It frequently feels more and more useful to withdraw into our shell. Instead, set aside that try and apprehend what is vital for your existence.

Concentrate on your goals. Consider what makes you pleased. By retaining your dreams alive, it is going to offer you a motive and potential to have a examine a compass at the fantastic manner to make the changes you want to maintain on with a superior existence. If you do now not, you'll spend the the relaxation of your existence drifting via it absurdly with none goals, manner, middle, or cause.

You should likewise understand that social assistance is vital to what befalls you. Find strategies, of all patterns and sizes, to help other human beings via engaging inside the humanitarian try, be a listening ear for a accomplice in trouble, spend time with a creature or accomplish some thing outstanding for any character.

Make a Vision Board

As a teenager, you standard that some aspect grow to be capacity. You can also get lost in myth land constantly. You had been proficient at imagining and envisioning what you will be at the identical time as you grew up.

We, as a whole, lose that capability as we form into maturity. Your worries and mind get blanketed up thru the responsibilities you get, and also you begin to overlook or be given that wearing out your goals is incredible.

Making a Vision Board is an incredible impetus as a manner to begin conducting and confiding in your goals yet again and imagining your desires every day on a imaginative and prescient board will breathe life into quality changes. We, at that issue, begin to agree with inside the danger of making them exercise session as predicted.

Be Positive

You cannot constrain your self to have a few correct instances or experience pride, however you could pressure your self to do certain topics, regardless of whether you do not experience find it irresistible.

Regardless of whether or not alternate does now not leave away proper now, you can bite via bit feel higher and an increasing number of enthusiastic to make time to concentrate on preparations as opposed to problems.

Practice contemplation. It can help lessen disappointment, lower the pressure you've got were given gathered, and lift high-quality emotions, happiness, and prosperity. Reward your self with moments of pleasure and famend and show appreciation as quickly as an afternoon.

It is one of the processes to alternate your lifestyles for the higher. You ought no longer to miss a few awesome moments because of the fact you are too bustling concentrating on your problems raised by using alternate.

Set Goals

When your fancy life seems alive all over again, you need to make a fixed and flow lengthy-haul, short-term goals and medium. It is following up on the ones targets that empower you to perform a exchange to enhance topics.

Keep in mind your life might also change as activities take area all at once. However, you want to continually be adaptable in enhancing your sails with the breeze that blows and don't forget the ones changes.

The little advances that you are creating a drift for alternate to occur on your life.

Experience Knowledge

When you revel in or advantage a few new useful understanding, you decorate your statistics and with it come more reality. It makes you regularly flexible and adaptable to specific circumstances in your lifestyles.

Accordingly, with the aid of way of way of escaping your everyday form of familiarity, you get steadily all proper with the obscure.

Perusing books is an notable path that allows you to analyze. You need to in no manner stop searching and getting greater knowledge because it gives your lifestyles because of this that and to alternate your life, it's miles beneficial.

Try no longer to Have Regrets

You have to apprehend that regrets are sports of the past and in case you spend some time considering it, you could pass over remarkable things within the gift as what is to go back is not yet composed.

You recognize you can't trade what you in all likelihood did or didn't do in beyond instances, so permit it circulate. The essential detail you have got control over is the manner you maintain on at the side of your gift and destiny existence.

Here is a sincere method to dispose of regrets: Get some inflatables and explode them. At that factor, compose on every honestly considered one among them a aspect you lamented and in a while allow them to bypass as you spot them going off into the sky, bid farewell to those regrets for eternity.

Deal with Your Fears

If you want to change your lifestyles for higher, you want to determine out the way to rule your emotions of dread in order that they can not have manage over you anymore. They are without a doubt musings you region in your thoughts which aren't right; you actually be for the reason that they'll be legitimate.

You need to apprehend that it is your apprehensions in lifestyles that save you you from sporting on collectively along side your life without limit. Be that as it can, even as you face your emotions of dread, you reclaim your capability to pick out and select the manner you need to hold on together along with your lifestyles and even as to do that, you do trade your life for eternity.

You ought to make a rundown of demanding things which you can likely form of want to do but are excessively hesitant to. Set up an association and make a glide to do them.

Think Differently

Try now not to sum up your terrible encounters. Think alternatively, "I can perform a little factor I positioned my mind to."

Try not to look subjects in darkish or white. Think as an opportunity, "I fizzled, but subsequent time I won't."

Try now not to lessen the exquisite of a circumstance. Think rather "She said as a good deal, and I consider it."

Notice every one of the things that went proper in preference to the matters that grew to come to be out badly.

Try not to shape a hasty opinion with the resource of means of creating fake understandings without genuine evidence.

Try no longer to surely be for the reason that the way you experience right presently displays reality. Think rather, "I realize I am a victor!"

Never, underneath any instances, call your self inadequately. State as an opportunity, "I'm headed, and I am justified, no matter all the hassle!"

Try not to hold your self to what you need to and ought not to do.

To close to, you need to realise that the primary character who is going to make a change to your existence is you and without a doubt you. So now, I leave you with a desire to make, at the manner you want to trade your life for better. If you are making a circulate on my message, stop ifs, ands or buts from your thoughts-set and alternate your existence till the give up of time.

xChange Your Life By Visualizing

When humans are keen on developing a noteworthy lifestyles exchange, it thoroughly may be alarming. Most of the population is impervious to alternate due to the fact they take a look at the difference with torment. I'm going to impart to you an incredible journey a good way to alternate that obvious torment, into the direct inverse - a few factor that makes you experience tremendous.

It's known as visualizing.

Visualizing the way you want to live is one of the pleasant processes to noticeably exchange your existence.

If you're new to this exercising, I'll provide you with a have a look at forthright you also can experience marginally awkward from the begin. We're delivered up in truth as we are aware of it modified into visualizing, or wandering off in myth land, or fantasizing about what we need is typically disliked. How frequently have to you be capable of go through in thoughts wandering off in myth land in university, and the educator guided you to rouse and focus?

In any case, what is so misconstrued approximately visualizing is that it receives you to in that you need to be. The kids that had been determined wandering off in delusion land in elegance are comparable kids which may be presently wearing on with the existence they longed for each this kind of years lower lower back.

Our minds are powerful. Each time we've were given interaction an concept in our mind, it sends our frame into the regarding vibration, and, because of this, we follow up on that vibration. Fundamentally, our thoughts manipulate our feelings, and our feelings dictate our movements. If you query this, take a gander at the monetary unrest that this kind of large massive shape of people are encountering in recent times. They have time-venerated thoughts of lack and constraint to dictate how they'll be feeling - misplaced, bewildered, and terrified. Since they will be on this horrific vibration, they act in techniques that guarantee more loss of their lifestyles. They reduce again on their fees. They keep themselves in an profession they are depressing doing. They cannot see an go out plan because their fact is considered considered considered one of lack.

If they had been no longer feeling such dread, they might never once more be restrained. If they determined out that the whole universe changed into successfully to be had, they could apprehend that they're chargeable for all elements of their lifestyles. They could no longer fear the economic system or stay in an profession they detest. They should recognise that lone they manipulate their life - now not each person or some issue else. They might apprehend that they control their very very private money owed, and they manage their pleasure. So they could think plenteous, happy, lifestyles-giving thoughts, which purpose them to feel the ones brilliant emotions, and they act in fine ways that improve their existence.

Have you at any problem visible which you assume in photographs? If we do not forget some issue, an photograph is anticipated in our mind, and we will see that concept. Think about the vehicle you strength, the kitchen you are making your dinners in, or the bed in that you hit the hay. Think about inner a cinema, retaining up in line on the air terminal, or going to a soccer healthy-up. In a everyday progression, those pix fly into your mind - you can see each honestly considered one in every of this stuff.

So, because of the fact we assume in photos, it permits us to bridle this energy of visualizing. We can honestly snap the image we find out in our thoughts and transform it into the physical form in our truth.

Choosing what you want is substantial. It need to be clear. Generally, this exercising won't give you amazing results. You in all likelihood might not get any results. You need to virtually plunk down and make sense of what you need from existence and the way you need to stay - all factors of it. From the kind of house you need to the shape of mate you need, in the form of shoes you can put on, to the day by day life-style you will lead - take a couple of minutes and document everything. The greater detail you placed into this picture of your new existence, the better your effects is probably.

Since you've got got an less expensive photo of the form of lifestyles you want to stay, in all its grand wonder, you need to consume this image into your mind. So, close to your eyes, and begin to visualize the image you just recorded.

It is vital to do that unfiltered. I do not get your because of this with the useful resource of unfiltered? Indeed, assume some part of your new existence makes them own a few issue big, you may ponder internally, "I claim a incredibly clean and trendy a few element. I love riding it down the roadway in entire extravagance and pleasure as I experience its power flood inside the route of me." That is the way you want to count on at the same time as you visualize the lifestyles which you want.

The separated variation of this idea might be something along the traces of, "One day I may additionally claim that especially costly some element that I haven't any clue how I will endure."

Do you see the distinction? In the two times, you're placing your emotions into the picture - it truly is crucial to this workout. In any case, you want to make contributions in truth high-quality feelings, not poor ones.

The unfiltered concept is your preference in its most satisfactory shape, at the equal time as, the sifted idea is your preference with barriers. If you begin setting aside your goals, the image you're visualizing will in no manner appear due to the reality you will make contributions terrible feelings and visualizing the lack in location of specializing in power and abundance. So, apprehend if you start to try this and save you it from gaining out of electricity. Remember, you are on pinnacle of things of your existence.

To visualize efficiently, you need to be separated from genuinely truely all and sundry else together along with your thoughts. There isn't any arranging this. So, execute all distractions - your telephone, the television, the sound machine, the PC - some thing in an effort to make your thoughts meander. You might choose no longer to warfare to listen what the universe is making an attempt to provide you.

As you don't forget your new life, sense the entirety about it. Feel the good. Feel the love. Feel your self being content material with the whole thing in your lifestyles. If you want a circle of relatives, be content material cloth how satisfied you are that you have a family. If you want to maintain your very very very

very own enterprise business enterprise, revel in the precise pleasure due to the reality you could win your very personal cash, time permitting, engaging in a few element you want to do.

Numerous human beings visualize themselves BECOMING this character they need to be - and this is a hundred% off base. If you take into account your self getting to be, you will normally be manifesting a circumstance of having to be. You want to believe as despite the fact that you're as of now that individual and proper now carrying on with that lifestyles because of the truth this is the issue an outstanding way to circulate into the shape. Remember at the equal time as you were a toddler, and also you imagined you had been a worldwide-beauty competitor or a well-known artist? This is the equal.

You'll need to try this workout for a couple of minutes in any event as quickly as every day - instances if you could. You can't receive the strength that you may release when you start to visualize your new life often.

To recap, first, you need to represent what you want. At that point, visualize somewhere wherein you're undisturbed, and in fact revel in your natural, unfiltered choice of this new lifestyles. When you are finished, you'll revel in your frame in a vibration of strength and pleasure. It is that this vibration so that you can dictate what you do, and the results you may get. By visualizing often, you will trade your life quicker, and similarly comfortable than you may have ever anticipated.

Use A Sick Day To Change Your Life

Sick days are a chunk of lifestyles. You can allow yourself to be overpowered with unhappiness, reprimand yourself for the entirety you might not entire, and fear every muscle because the minute's cruise thru. You can likewise make use of the day to invigorate yourself, to loosen up your worn-out body, and to change your lifestyles. Your reaction to contamination includes a desire if you will part of the good deal and pressured, or energetic and content cloth. Here are ten strategies to make a sick day effective and worthwhile. In what manner will your next sick day exchange your life?

Create a outstanding frame of mind. Did you understand that outstanding, enthusiastic states and sound pressure the executives can help your insusceptibility? An research with the useful resource of using the University of Wisconsin-Madison (Davidson 2004) recommends folks that react with excellent emotions have precise thoughts motion produced by means of way of way of these feelings that expands insusceptibility. Following up from awesome investigations that show the frame of thoughts will have an impact on your nicely-being, this precise examination preferred to recognise why. The scientists predicted antibodies created in the wake of accepting an influenza immunization and positioned an enlargement inside the resistant response for the folks who had a high quality entire of feeling style. React to existence truly, and you may be extra healthy. How must you deal with the stress of disappointment or the surprising? Make sure you have got what it takes to compartmentalize your feelings and placed everything into problem of view. When you're unwell, you want to allow your frame to combat. Make certain you win the combat in mind.

You could be healthier if your mind thinks precious and uplifting musings. When you're unwell in mattress is not the time to remember each one of the property you can not do. Instead, set up with your self to contemplate what you CAN do.

As critical as you're on your commitments, deliver your self consent to be human. This does not advise which you drop the entirety on every occasion there may be any trace of a sniffle, but do not be at the possibility notable, directing workplace artwork on the identical time as being triaged at a hospital. Life is a careful exercise in cautious manage.

Live it with a ardour that starts offevolved with a greater match body of thoughts.

1. Offer your self a reprieve. Your frame desires rest at the identical time as you're unwell. Sustain it and get invigorated. Treat your self to the gentlest tissue you could discover on your sore nostril. Get the maximum agreeable pads and covers, and discover your chosen spot to curl up and rest. Enable others to don't forget you, and be thankful if you have cherished ones round to assist. Unplug your self from the arena. When you're immensely throbbing and requiring rest, flip off your phones, and special far off gadgets. If you need to hold one on for crises, brush aside it except if it's miles a actual disaster (clue: visitor identification).

2. Revise your goals. Think approximately the rundown of stresses or undertakings whirling round for your mind, and after that, do that psychological exercise. If you have got been to kick the bucket this unique on the spot, what can also anyhow count quantity?

Whatever is presently unimportant may be dispose of until the next day. Quit considering it now. For those errands which is probably as yet vital for the afternoon, delegate them proper away. Complete the well-knownshows early and after that, decide to dismiss them. If you're involved approximately the final outcomes, located people you agree with answerable for managing the whole lot you have got special with the purpose that they might do the stressing. Presently unwind.

three. Fight it. Be resolved to overcome it as speedy as time permits. If you cannot physical upward thrust up, you may, anyhow, advantage amazing things together together with your mind. Choose to make the day taken into consideration taken into consideration one in every of success. When you're keen, in vicinity of consuming in mattress, sit in which you generally devour. A trade of room can assist carry a gradually notable thing of view. After you start to feel surprisingly rested, scrub down.

four. Utilize the time your frame is resting to take an individual inventory. It is higher to speak about this which you are content together along with your life? Is it accurate to say that something is worrying you? Are there any regions for self-interest and improvement? Is it authentic that you are viably handling your stress and a while, or may additionally you have the capability to utilize a few higher-adapting aptitudes for better fulfillment? Is your existence seminar heading within the right course? Pick 3 subjects, and pick out out to build up your boldness and create a superior you via confronting them. Did you understand that many maintain in mind burnout to be a hole amongst your goals and your praise (Farber 1983)? What do you anticipate that isn't happy? As you begin feeling better, plan some factor to assignment out. It may additionally unique some stressful words to any person. It may be starting a diary to can help you comply with lifestyles. You might possibly want to peruse an exceptional ebook or peruse the net for research and handy tips.

You can also get the fearlessness to start a corporation, exercise for some unique characteristic, or move lower lower back to magnificence.

five. Assess your otherworldly existence. Is it easy to mention that you are content material with your self inside the lonely instances, or does the calm cause disrupting feelings to ground? Is it clean to say that you are awesome approximately your convictions approximately God and your association with Him, or is vulnerability growing inconvenience? Supplicate, look at the Bible, or track in. Spend a

6. portion of your loosening up day being a console to your spirit via the use of the writer of solace. If you expel the existence of God on your life precept, appoint this time to don't forget in case you are taking the defects of others and crediting them to God. He is not the writer of your torment, however He is the person who can will can help you get out of it. I regard you reserve the option to differ with

me that God exists; however, ensure which you are first-rate about your alternatives.

7. Stay on course. Try not in price your contamination for being wrecked from your manner in lifestyles. If you have got been eating nicely, at that difficulty, keep doing it. Because you can eat crackers for a while does not recommend you need to make up for all of the lost suppers at the same time as you revel in like eating another time. When you're better, stay privy to the obligations you made previously. If you keep away from touchy sugars (as someone does), at that point affably divulge to the coolest-natured companions, who america you want Jell-o or Gatorade that you are doing fine and dandy at any rate. There is sans sugar Jell-o if you should have it, with every one of the synthetics that includes. If you avoid liquor, at that issue, do now not take Nyquil (which has 10% liquor). There are some of virus capsules handy if feature remedy alternatives are not your inclination.

I pursue an ingesting plan which has helped me live in recovery from my ingesting problem for added than 14 years now. It includes eating adjusted sustenances approximately each 4-five hours and maintaining in mind that there are adaptability and collection, she has a base and maximum immoderate she want to flavor for each putting. This liberates me and encourages me deliberately abstain from setting my emotions into nourishment. When she modified into sick and incapable to devour, that doesn't propose she modified into off my plan. She will no longer be wrecked. Here is one stunt she utilizes which could let you comprehend in case you are endeavoring to veer off base. If she end up surely ready to consume crackers from the begin, at that issue, so be it. She reveals whilst she starts offevolved offevolved offevolved to enjoy better, she also can ponder internally "properly, she as but unwell, so she need to feel loose to consume an entire package deal deal of crackers due to the fact it might consolation/unwinding/amusing, and pressure over adjusting it later." This is a warning for me, and she or he or he or he speedy realizes that if she wants to justify it, and make use of an emotive phrase ("comforting,..."), at that component she was all right to devour higher. She might not be organized to consume a serving of blended vegetables, but she may be capable of certainly add some top notch nutritional classes to my dinner. Furthermore, at the same time as sick, protein is high-quality for assisting the frame re-benefit power.

What is it you justify within the wake of being sick? It is simple to say that you are thinking about preventing your interest device genuinely because you had to bypass over an afternoon? Is it regular to say that you had been persuaded even as attaining some close to the residence intention, and will you are saying you're currently enticed to toss it aside? Fight to stay at the proper music and prop up for your voyage. You are justified, irrespective of all the trouble!

1. Start some different addiction or damage a terrible one. Why take a seat tight for New Year's goals? Utilize your ill day to begin new. Have you perception approximately the impacts of your vital espresso? Besides the monetary price of a scrumptious Starbuck's healing, there may be a actual price. You have maximum likely officially encountered the caffeine withdrawal manifestations (low power, cerebral pain, and so forth) for the duration of your contamination. Why move back? Push beforehand. Have you desired to surrender cigarettes, and find that your body rejected them at the identical time as ill? Try no longer to enhance them all over again for enthusiastic reasons; however, take benefit of your unwell day and begin a searching for plan. Have you desired to begin practising or ingesting higher? Utilize the time to create a plan for even as you enjoy better. You may moreover additionally discover that feeling so awful creates a few enthusiasm for the possibility of feeling so pinnacle. Spur yourself and pick out out at any charge one addiction to break or start. At that component, do it.

2.   Dream. What may additionally you do if you can exchange your life? Utilize your sick day, a day ride of your run of the mill agenda, to keep in thoughts your existence path. Set dreams and element excessive. Prepare to stun the arena. It may be very well; no one will snicker. Furthermore, no man or woman may also realize if you live calm. Consider telling someone your desires, dreams, and goals. You may additionally moreover locate consolations in notable spots. At that factor, make a circulate. Is it better to mention which you are left with an all- encompassing contamination? Think about how you can make use of the time to help different people. The maximum remarkable malignant boom pledge drives start with one individual thinking about what to do to impact the world. Shouldn't a few aspect be stated approximately you?

3.   Develop, create, and grow. Before your day is completed, beautify your life. Discover some new statistics. Watch a narrative or "the manner to" seem on tv. Peruse a ebook about

a subject you do now not have the foggiest idea about. Peruse the web to understand what you do now not commonly search out. Assess your life cause, your percentage of fulfillment, and don't forget your effective obtain. Create a submit in your blog when you have one, or supply what dreams be via something medium your capacity lets in. You may be enormously useful even as your frame rests. You may even trade your lifestyles. Do it these days.

Chapter 3: Optimism Is Good For You

What is optimism?

Optimism is an idea firmly identified with happiness. It is ready no longer surrendering at the same time as conditions become truely difficult. However, on the identical time as the going is proper, having optimism implies you assume that the exceptional must continue. It is tied in with having an expectation, and constantly accepting subjects will enhance. Being an optimist locations you in an exceptional characteristic to deal with conditions to your life and to address life's problems for the most element.

As a rule:

Optimists take transport of horrible subjects are brief. They once in a while upward push up (instead of usually) and might not final. For example, your manager yelling at you on Monday does no longer imply they may yell at you for the rest of your going for walks lifestyles. An optimist has a mindfulness that horrible matters will stand up in life.

However, they may upward push up over again while the terrible takes region. It implies they may count on duty for their lifestyles, in location of choosing not to problem, as what's the fact, it's miles the whole thing going to expose out terrible anyhow.

Bad activities aren't their shortcoming. For example, the horrible weather conditions made it hard to win. It is easy guilty yourself unreasonably. However, everyday self-blame can damage yourself assurance if you may take a gander at brilliant motives you will be predisposed to, along side your self better. You need to be in rate of your actions; besides, your reasoning have to be realistic. An optimist does not obviously blame themselves whilst something appears badly.

Optimists preserve horrible activities to that one specific state of affairs. For example, because you ignored one birthday, does not purpose them to neglectful in all elements of their life. You coincidentally forgot that one birthday. If terrible things get up, it isn't always the part of the affiliation and can additionally be taken into consideration as issues to be triumph over. Optimists do not overdramatize the circumstance.

Interestingly:

Optimists count on that proper events want to closing. For example, heating the correct cake - they do not do not forget this to be a unique case. They are an top notch cake maker; accordingly, their cakes are continuously proper. Interestingly, even as optimists be successful, they will be predisposed to invest extra power next time, as a end result making success greater probable.

Right occasions are in their very own making and are due to their capacities and developments. This mind-set can serve to make you experience suitable about yourself. It method taking a high-quality function of probabilities after they emerge and having the fearlessness to threat — for example, having the braveness to capture up a functionality vocation possibility, rather than dismissing it and at last passing up a large possibility.

For optimists, suitable things come to have an impact on first rate areas of their lifestyles truly. It improves all that they do considering they revel in excellent approximately themselves. For instance, fulfillment at artwork improves your thoughts-set to your property lifestyles. They do not kingdom they arise to be a amazing bookkeeper (and they may be no longer a lot that particular, it's miles without a doubt no character else wants to carry out the responsibility) but the relaxation of their existence is a wreck.

How is optimism remarkable?

Physical properly-being

There are right properly-being motivations to be splendid. Research demonstrates optimists have more grounded resistant frameworks, making them a whole lot much less powerless to contamination and infection. They are a super deal much less inclined to chunk the dirt of a coronary coronary heart assault or cardiovascular infection. Other studies demonstrates that an nice mind-set implies you may get nicely faster from an hobby. Optimists have a good deal much less pressure, which averts many stress-associated scientific problems, and it's far proposed them at ultimate stay more.

An thrilling trouble approximately optimists is that they may be certain to discover a way to avoid infection and rush to get treatment at the equal time as contamination strikes.

Emotional fitness

Optimism can be an tremendous truth promoter when you remember that it could give you a feel of manipulate for your life. It can enhance your brand new prosperity. The studies did via Seligman emphatically demonstrates that optimists have plenty tons much less melancholy. Optimism can forestall you feeling prone, it really is an critical purpose of misery. Optimists were proved to be grade by grade successful in all regular problems, along facet paintings, sports activities activities, and connections.

How optimism can assist?

Optimism is a mind-set. It is simply the contemplations you u . S . As quickly as a day at the same time as you revel in precise situations. Your musings can amazingly affect your lifestyles. Thinking with a bit of achievement empowers you to pleasure inside the proper matters and conquer the incorrect stuff. In that ability, it gives you the important idea to accomplish your goals, every massive and little. Odds are you can benefit extra, as an effective attitude will provide you with the pressure to hold onward. After fulfillment, an optimist will invest greater power, finally prompting greater fulfillment. They do no longer positioned fulfillment all of the way all the way right down to karma, possibility, or one-of-a-kind outer influences. It can absolutely resource you without hesitation as you apprehend the alternatives you have got and the amount you could do in conjunction with your lifestyles.

Optimism, similar to happiness, is not a few mystical marvel that keeps bad topics from taking area. It does besides provide you with the threat to stumble upon extraordinary stuff for a extra awesome degree of time and be in a scenario to address the horrible topics in a pleasing, appealing way.

One may say that a part of negativity continues us grounded, yet optimism can flood us forward. . They do now not placed fulfillment all of the way all the manner all the way down to karma, possibility, or different outer impacts. It can genuinely useful resource you with out hesitation as you understand the picks you have got were given and the quantity you can do along side your life.

How to Succeed by using manner of Creating a Definite effect in Your Life

There is a huge form of steps which can be critical to gain achievement via growing a excellent exchange in your lifestyles. Our "gift" is generally stuffed via the use of in reality one in all topics. This is, we both little by little maintain close to the past, or we live up for our future. While it's far proper to be privy to the past, surely as to the destiny, we ought to make each push to do as such in a wonderful and beneficial manner. Reflection and expectation are fruitful for us at the same time as we are:

"Taking the eye of the beyond, using it to our present, with an cease intention to make a successful and profitable destiny"

In this guide, you'll be familiar with a way to be successful close to developing a first-rate trade in your lifestyles. You will decide out a manner to look the beyond as a extremely good gathering of cognizance, observe that knowledge inside the "now," and make your very very own clever give up cease end result for the future. If you've got noted that a change need to be made, and you are prepared to begin authorizing that alternate for your life, you need to keep perusing. If you have not recounted that a trade need to be made, and you are geared up to move... All things taken into consideration, no place. You want to give up perusing right away right here and grapple with the manner that stagnation is not whatever above a rearing pit for disappointment.

Desire

To advantage close to growing a trade in our lives, it is essential to need to exchange. That is to mention, and you want to have a honest preference. If you're changing due to the fact you figure it'll make every other character help of you more, or which includes you more, you need to avoid returned up to that "stagnation" spill. You can in no way in truth CHANGE besides if YOU need the exchange, and feature a true choice for it. If the idea of trade is grade by grade near home and vital to you, you're very vulnerable to be increasingly diligent in searching for after it. It is moreover vital to guarantee which you bear in mind the "benefits and drawbacks" of the exchange which you need to make in your life in advance than commencing on the journey to acquire it.

Capacity

Presently, as you center throughout the trade which you want to gain for your lifestyles, you must bear in mind your capability to carry out the transformation. As it have been, is the trade which you need to make sensibly talking? If it isn't moderately speaking, you could find out your self beaten with complete and specific dissatisfaction. It is idea and perceptive that there may be a positive level of "fact" that should be confronted almost about exchange. We as a whole love those outwardly attractive styles of adjustments that make us revel in all stunning and gung ho, but in all fact, there are some modifications which may be low-cost and a few so that you can result in steady dissatisfaction because of the way that they are no longer internal our functionality.

Positive Thinking

Indeed, I am going to expose to you that the depth of super questioning will make you a success on the subject of creating a trade in your life. I apprehend, I realise... You have got heard the whole lot previously. Wouldn't you are saying there can be a few degree of legitimacy to this advice if it's so "fashionable"? Honestly, you need to hold your musings proper away with reference to achieving change. How may additionally you make a exchange and believe in it if you continually count on which you cannot? Did you ever prevent and don't forget in case you are wondering which you can not say which you are the primary person keeping you over from all that you may involvement in lifestyles? If now not, you want to consider this. Stay high-quality, and you are probable going to be very a success!

Patience and Support

Patience and assist are of the primary basics in terms of prevailing with a exchange on your existence. To start with, you want to parent out how to build up a touch staying power for the transition to appear. We as a whole, hear, "alternate does not appear overnight." I do no longer apprehend exactly how a great deal reality there can be in that assertion because of the fact I do get maintain of that change can display up in a unmarried day. It won't be the huge aim that you have your factors of hobby set on. However, honestly the choice to make a exchange is a exchange - what did that take you, all of 5 mins if that? The key's being expertise at the same time as it's far going to the closing outcomes. We want to bear in thoughts it... Not very many "clever fruits" have been made in a day. Aren't you a magnum opus? Obviously! We as an entire are! Take as an entire lot time as essential and get the traces, the shapes, and the colors proper. You may be satisfied which you did!

Support is some other important component in terms of developing a change for your lifestyles. There is a massive form of sorts of help that you can come upon while trying to make a alternate. The secret's to "preserve in thoughts new thoughts." How about we see, loved ones are awesome manual frameworks. Expert advising and training assets are exquisite, as nicely! Enjoy one, revel in all! You absorb as lots assist as you could. Keep in mind, the team that has the most game enthusiasts is regularly the team that leads the percent in any actual assignment. Amazing a collection - a team on the way to will let you win whilst growing a exchange to your lifestyles!

Positive Psychology What it's far and How to Use It?

In the good 'old days, psychology become for the maximum element about research. They had to see how reflexes labored (touch warm variety... Ouch! Allow your hand be moved away), declaration worked (I see an older person... Presently I see a princess...) and the manner conduct labored (hound sees nourishment... It salivates). When psychology started, it had three points: address and be a part of intellectual sickness, assist 'innovative genius' or wonders which within the ones days also can had been pressured with intellectual contamination, and assist each day human beings stay higher lives.

The intellectual contamination become a mainstream element after WWII and WWI. Psychologists who play in labs and permit addresses during the day had new vocation openings. They need to deal with people who have been returning domestic from conflict tormented by mental contamination. What's extra, poof... A ton of financing and cash-filled reading a way to repair what wasn't right with human beings. Well in 2008, we currently understand A LOT approximately what's up with people. We have medicines for max highbrow ailments or even a few fixes. We moreover apprehend a awesome deal approximately contemporary genius; but, in famous, psychology did not understand a ton about your constantly. Joe Seligman went through the majority of his time inside the world studying melancholy and examined that depression is determined out. At that problem he asked, must no longer a few thing be said about nicely faith? For a long time, psychologists believed that in case you took an individual who come to be discouraged and eliminated their despair, you may have a happy person. However, that isn't always legitimate. Because you do no longer have a cold, would now not imply you are preferably strong.

Because you are not discouraged does no longer imply you experience active, euphoric and love your life. The hassle of tremendous psychology on occasion alluded to due to the fact the have a examine of happiness makes use of the identical clinical meticulousness that has been associated with reading what goes on with humans and the way to restoration them, to statistics the broadness of human potential.

Positive psychologists lead research on such things as self belief, versatility, coarseness, consider, bliss, amazement, traits, happiness, circulate, supplication, and silliness. Anybody can have a look at the studies that has left outstanding psychology into their lives and vocations. Specialists, as an example, psychologists, advisors and lifestyles mentors, employ high-quality psychology to discover what is as of now taking walks with customers and assist them collect their tendencies, discover determination and significance of their lifestyles.

They assist them sense happier and frequently happy. Positive psychology is unique than "luckily." We are not supporting humans to be happy, satisfied, satisfied commonly. It's critical to feel angry, dissatisfied, and dismal while it's miles suitable.

That is emotion every one of the emotions that human creatures count on in choice to trying to reveal to ourselves we ought to be happy normally. It's tied in with permitting your self to feel all remarkably up with out stalling out. For a long term, psychology did now not authorize human beings to be human. The location become intensely slanted on highbrow infection; extraordinary psychology is tied in with night time day out the scale.

Bringing as a whole lot interest to the excessive fantastic component of lifestyles as we should the terrible. The studies leaving powerful psychology is fascinating. At no other time have researchers ran twofold daze fake remedy ponders on things like happiness, appreciation, and precise faith. Presently, you might imagine, why attempt directing a studies be aware of find out that doing correct matters for others can can help you experience better? I concur with you. Innately we apprehend those matters are actual and we have to do this. Be that as it is able to, what number of hopeless or marginally sad humans do you run over to your life? What range of people do you understand that make a unique attempt to carry out some component respectable for some distinct individual?

Far superior, make a unique effort for a whole outsider? Research indicates that you could significantly and short beautify your happiness diploma absolutely by means of the usage of wearing out some thing decent for every unique individual. These humans are happier, have better connections, are regularly loved thru others, and feel better approximately themselves. Indeed, we realize that doing these objects can profits our lives. Be that as it can, we neglect. Or as an alternative, we do no longer apprehend the impact it may have on us. Sound clinical research is incredible stuff. An examination showed that profits reps who've a have a look at capabilities on wearing out stronger and hopeful had been 3 times more powerful than their discouraged partners.

If you're an corporation proprietor, that may be a big ordeal. Research suggests that taking detail in art work that empowers you to utilize your features and what you are typically top at empowers you to be happier further to frequently possible. Makes feel, right? However, what several humans do you recognize that get the opportunity to do what they may be actual at and like to do every day? Positive psychology is extremely good from self-improvement and pop psychology.

Its organizer Martin Seligman is assured that incredible psychology need to be spellbinding, rather than prescriptive. Which manner, in desire to analyzing what expands happiness and in a while telling people a manner to manipulate their lives, exceptional psychology need to portray the studies on these points. As in line with Seligman, human beings lead sound investigations on factors, for example, flexibility, appreciation, and petition, make experience of the manner these items have an impact on people and the components via which they art work.

At that issue, they educate people what the studies shows. For instance, thinks approximately showcase that speaking builds your experience of exceptional feelings and reduces the aspect consequences of depression. Appreciative people are regularly idealistic about destiny events, enjoy an increasing number of related to others, or maybe document higher satisfactory rest. As researchers direct the ones examinations, they plan to understand the additives associated with appreciation: how can it paintings? Why does it art work?

Positive analyst nation, "display human beings the research, help them make informed choices about what could probably artwork superb in their lifestyles." This is ground-breaking and drastically amazing from endorsing or telling people a manner to live their lives. As a nice psychology-primarily based lifestyles mentor, I consolidate each a captivating and a prescriptive method. I portray superb psychology- based techniques for making the extraordinary change customers need to look, and I make recommendations depending on what has labored for me and others.

As a discipline, excessive excellent psychology has taken off. Simply Google "happiness" + "have a have a take a look at" and take a gander at how plenty happiness has been in the media as of late. Attempt words like flexibility, euphoria, humor, trends, coarseness, life satisfaction, and you could see that high-quality psychology is speedy extending. The formal that means of exquisite psychology, a l. A. Wikipedia, is "the scientific investigation of the developments and ethics that empower human beings and networks to flourish." Every month there can be an ever-growing kind of charming examinations turning out in the problem. We have scarcely began out to reveal what we realise to be the ones functions and beliefs; anyhow, excellent psychology is changing people's lives across the arena.

If we are not developing we're deteriorating

If we aren't developing, we're weakening.It is human intuition to keep growing, maintain getting to know to keep enhancing. We don't have any acquaintance with the entirety. We, as a whole, have bodily sports to investigate. I'm speculating which you would really like to decorate your existence because of the truth you are perusing this, or possibly you need to alternate everything about your revel in. If your scenario is at that point, do not give up due to the truth there can be a 'thump on' effect.

When you convert your reasoning, and you change one thing to your lifestyles, then everything else will comply with.:-) Maybe it's miles your interest you need to trade, or your fee variety, your courting, weight, self-notion, fitness or perhaps the entirety appears ideal however something is missing, however you cannot recognize why you are as however ?

The element is we enjoy existence harping on what we're discontent with, grumble approximately those subjects and permit them to make us extensively gradually hopeless. Every so frequently we may moreover try to attend to them, yet we lose middle, and it would not keep going fairly lengthy (at any issue made a New Year's Resolution?)after which we beat ourselves up for 'arising short,' and the cycle begins.

There are superb topics we need to remember in advance than we are able to exchange. There are likewise matters we should do after we have made Strides One. These preliminary degrees are fairly normal reasons we flop so now you realize next time you may be successful.

Stage One

Choose WHAT you want! Who would possibly you want to be? How might also want to you want to revel in? (Truly, its a desire, you can experience it now if making a decision to) What do you want to do? Where may you want to transport?

Be particular. Consider it cautiously, write it down and look at it every morning and each night time. This will preserve you centered.

When you've got a take a look at it enjoy the feelings, you will have if you as of now have it, press the enthusiasm and the pride, and the appreciation.

Stage 2

Make a Decision, a proper 100% strength of mind! Not, oh, I need I had that. Make a assure to yourself, a pledge, that is the difficulty that I will do, and I can do it! The most critical piece of this is you FEEL appropriate. Feeling terrible about your trouble/scenario or your self will make you feel greater awful and the issue more regrettable. (See The Secret Explained). Begin to enjoy engaged and excellent, excited, and incredible determined, and absolutely glad.

You advantage it; you may do it!

Be benevolent to your self, your declare closest accomplice. Feeling responsible makes you hopeless, and the factor proper right here is to revel in proper. Lose the blame forestall beating yourself for not being awesome and highlight on all this is right about you and your intention. Enormous yourself up! Harp for your abilities and the subjects you want about your self. If you can't don't forget any you actually need to do that, ask a loved one what they love approximately you yet, please try to do it unbiased from all and sundry else first.

Keep in thoughts how awesome you're; that is why you ARE loved and cope with yourself as desires are. Alright, so now you have selected what you want and made a dedication to yourself that you'll accomplish it.

Stage 3

Accept. If there may be a query to your mind, then you without a doubt should dispose of it brief as this demonstrates disappointment is as but a preference, and it isn't always.

Our own ideals are original from start; they will be instilled into us through our mother and father, own family, friends, and encounters and make our belief of ourselves. They impact our mind, our feelings, our dreams, and our relationships and the manner we sense approximately ourselves. We should have super beliefs and ideals that preserve us down on what we surely can do. Our beliefs can supply us a roof that we take shipping of we can't get through.

They set out fashions for ourselves in our lives. They direct what we enjoy we gain and prefer this what we accomplish. Do you think there may be any wealthy person who coincidentally made their cash? No, they regular they deserved it and have been eager to extensively diagnosed no less, that doesn't recommend their beliefs/requirements are as excessive in a single-of-a-type parts in their lives, for instance, relationships, properly-being and so on.

Our beliefs set our measures; we need to simply accept that we DESERVE what we are attempting to find to have, that we're particular sufficient, that we're able to do it. We make reasons to ourselves concerning why we can't have it/do it. This stems from our ideals (and fear, however we are able to get to that some other time).

There isn't always any truth, in reality perception. What's greater, your notion is your conviction, and you may change your beliefs if you decide to, and after that, so trade your 'existence.'

Things being what they may be, How Do I Change My Beliefs?

Well, our prolonged haul imbued beliefs are set up in our subconscious mind, we are not through the usage of any approach aware of a huge a part of them. However, I believe that now you understand about this, you can begin to find out your very very own issue limiting beliefs, and in some time, you may most possibly trade them.

You may recognize that you rehash unique examples on your existence, in any zone, probably in relationships or with coins. These examples originate from poor beliefs we've got were given, and you could consider them via brooding about any tedious behavior you could have. It might be near domestic relationships; do you believe you studied decrease once more and experience as though your last couple of relationships have been as regardless of the reality which you went out with a similar man or woman again and again?

Or on the other hand, do you keep gaining coins but in no way seem to have any? Plunk down and document any restricting beliefs or examples you can understand and document why you may have created them.

This might be a clumsy exercising; but, it's far justified, no matter all the problem as if you have identified them, you may supplant them with new powerful ones. They are essentially bad thoughts we've got about ourselves and our lives, however, like I stated earlier than they're able to emerge out of our subconscious, so we need to build our attention to what we're genuinely wondering.

Stage 4

Changing your horrible ideals is the most dominant method to change your lifestyles. Regardless of whether you accept as true with you can or you wouldn't, you are able to maximum probably proper.

Take a gander at your web page of limiting ideals and redesign them into remarkable feelings, as an instance:

'Nothing I do is ever proper enough' alternate to 'I can accomplish something I pick!'

'You Have To Work So Hard And Suffer To Have Money" trade to 'Money Flows To Me Frequently and Easily.'

"I'm Fat" exchange to 'I'm a period.And I appearance Great!'

"All The Good Ones Are Taken" change to 'My first-class partner is offered, and I will meet them soon."

"Nobody Finds Me Attractive." alternate to "I am adorable, and I attract parents that are right for me."

"I'm Tired All Of The Time." change to 'I am constantly loaded with power.'

Yes, it feels weird from the start; but, preserve at it, and you may retrain your unconscious to simply accept as real with it, and after that, it will come into interest. Changing the mind, we've and the matters we u . S . A . To ourselves changes the way we sense, behave, and make a circulate. It likewise pulls in gadgets topics to us. Positive thoughts draw in excellent matters, and pessimism breeds cynicism. Always make it right right into a sturdy advantageous, the subconscious thoughts does no longer understand the terms 'no longer' and 'do now not,' so do not usa 'I may not do smoke any in addition' say 'I am a nonsmoker.'

Always u . S . (and determine) what you DO want and relinquish what you do no longer want.

Stage 5

Plan your voyage. What do you need to do? How could you're pronouncing you will accomplish your targets? What apparatuses do you need? What is your initial step? Make a go together with the drift. Do what wishes to be completed. Whatever you want to do, get beneficial aid from circle of relatives and companions, and look at your association.

In synopsis:

Take some factor you have got committed to do. Identify any restricting beliefs you have got regarding this aim. You DO have a few else you will have it as of now. Change that conviction right into a excellent. Accept that you DESERVE your goal.

Make an association. Make a bypass! Make nowadays day by day of alternate.

Chapter 4: Confident With An Unmistakable Vision

To Be Optimistic

How often have you ever ever ever heard the maxim "Is the glass 1/2 unfilled or half of entire"? This honest saying might also moreover have out of place its actual significance or end up a buzzword due to the truth it is so regularly stated. If we absolutely test its importance, we can also realize the energy of splendid thinking that exists in the ones phrases. It has the electricity to allow your life change, your business, your fitness, your vocation, and supply you in the direction of know-how each one in every of your goals in existence.

When one is assured, they've got a powerful attitude on lifestyles. This critical element for living allows us the self notion to just accept that times will end up well for us. This alleviates excessive stress that empowers advanced health, better overall performance, and advanced non-public delight.

Research has tested that high-quality humans have greater grounded insusceptible frameworks and are steadily impervious to ailments and chronic ailments.

I need to fight an contamination called lupus in the course of the previous 15 years. I am reminded each day of this possibly horrible contamination I even have when I obtain over to take my tablets every morning and night. It has been my effective questioning that has empowered me to live healthy. It is my idealism that keeps the disorder managed where it'd not meddle with my life. It has been my first-rate frame of thoughts that has kept me alive this a long manner.

To be positive requires a cognizant exertion. Although you could have your mantras or ordinary reminders of the way positive you want to be, the change wishes to show up from in the mind. It takes profound contemplation and self- assessment to really recognize why you're willing to pessimism and the way it continues us down in existence. In any case, while you do, you'll experience prepared to eliminate the hold that melancholy has on you.

When you're Optimistic

How you defend times and oneself communicate and self- clarifications you offer, determine how extremely good or critical you're. When you enjoy troubles en direction do you fall with annihilation, or do you discover a first-class detail from which to artwork?

When you are superb, no longer some thing holds you up. You have the dedication to endure no matter the barricades in advance. When one manner is blocked, you locate non-compulsory strategies to surmount them. You end up an exquisite hassle solver, locating solutions for any tricky condition. You bear in mind every to be as an possibility to be successful, surrendering each little bit of proof to find quantities of facts. You generally envision the tremendous outcome.

When you're notable, you are inspired and prepared for success. Your preference is converted into dreams, and also you devise plans for reaching the ones desires. You are all the greater prepared to exit on a limb to advantage the level of fulfillment you want. The excellent mind is continuously warning and organized for movement, curious, and aware.

When you're optimistic, you became a pioneer and perception amongst your buddies or the humans you've got interaction with. This is a few factor that normally happens. Your stage of self belief will go with the flow others to consider their techniques of hypothesis to encompass your constructive fashion. You will find that others go with the flow within the route of you due to the truth your brilliant thinking will enchantment to them.

Being a assured individual is a preference you need to be keen to make. Choose to endure in mind them to be as 1/2 of entire and now not half unfilled. If you want for a incredible final results, choose to think with a piece of good fortune to make that final results. How you observed makes a selection the successes in your destiny. If you are a worrier, your dreams will slightly be determined out. If you are a effective philosopher, the possibilities of carrying out your dreams are exceedingly elevated.

Remember what and the way you be given as true with the issue that you appeal to. Think with hopefulness and pull in effective effects.

It is secure to say that you are an Optimist?

So you presently apprehend that it is so essential to be positive. You recognize about the reality that it is so important in your fitness, your achievement, and your destiny. So how would probable if you are a assured person?

Optimistic human beings are:

Sure humans

Cheery, sprightly human beings

Positive people

Increasingly profitable human beings

High achievers

Healthier people

Confident with an unmistakable imaginative and prescient of factors to return lower back lower back

More completely glad humans

Stronger

You are efficiently loved with the aid of manner of others and exceptional to be near.

Spotlights on what they have got and not what they do no longer have

Not crucial of others

Empowering of others

Not successfully unsettled or involved

Self-inspired

Increasingly liberal humans

Eager about what they may be doing

Sometimes our degree of unique faith is a few component we amplify from our kids. Possibly you have got were given or had horrible or crucial guardians. Guardians, need to you're announcing you are making an constructive vicinity to your youngsters to flourish in?

Make a stride again and watch your lifestyles from a advanced view. Realize the amount of fulfillment you want to attain for you and your family in all regions of lifestyles. Make the choice to enhance the u . S . A . Of mind for your circumstance. Remember it's far a preference you need to make to be positive so that you can gain the fulfillment you benefit!

Do you consider you are an positive character? Are there regions you need to paintings on? Do you experience you want help? A lifestyles mentor assist you to in the beginning to your hopeful adventure.

Instructions to be Optimistic

I understand how difficult it very well, perhaps once in a while. We are besieged every day with thousands of terrible information. We simplest on occasion concentrate incredible facts. Any longer. It seems the precept reminiscences that procure charge determinations in the media are tragic, bad stories. So how may irrespective of the entirety we live optimistic?

Creating Positive Career Changes

You and I are lucky. We live in a global, rich wonderful outcomes. We can pick from a large series of occupations, and reserve the privilege to discover pride and private pleasure in our everyday paintings.

The truth which you stay in a unfastened society offers you the advantage to determine your destiny. You have as a first rate deal manipulate in figuring out in which you figure as you do in deciding on a spouse, a domestic, a car, or a domestic dog. Your desire of employments definitely is predicated upon the quantity you need to form your vocation, and what kind of exertion you are willing to spend to make the essential enhancements on your life.

If you are thinking about a vocation change, it's in all likelihood diagnosed with three motives:

1 - Personal - You need to trade your associations with others.

For instance, you could have decided that you're contradictory with the individuals in your industrial corporation employer. Maybe they have got unique interests than you, or they speak differently or have specific instructive foundations.

2 - Professional - You've decided the want to propel your vocation

For instance, you've got found that you might not arrive at your professional or specialized desires at your gift commercial enterprise employer; or that your headway is being obstructed thru the usage of any character who is progressively senior or all the extra politically organized; or that you are not getting the acknowledgment you gain; or which you and your organization are growing in exquisite tips; or that you are not being tested absolutely; in any other case you aren't being given the abilities you want to are looking for paintings in a while. Or alternatively, you have out of location enthusiasm for your allocated errands.

three- Situational - You are spurred with the useful resource of approach of different conditions that all add in your pride within the place of work. Possibly you're riding excessively a protracted way from domestic each day, you are overly compartmentalized in your responsibilities, you're pressured to excursion excessively, you are running the kind of large quantity of hours, or you're underneath numerous pressure. Possibly you need to transport to each other metropolis, or live wherein you're in desire to being moved?

Whatever your private, professional, or situational motives might be, you are propelled through manner of the desire to enhance your diploma of employee pleasure and make a notable exchange. You'd be astonished how many people are vague about what they accomplish professionally, and the way their occupations cause them to sense. To decipher your dreams and dreams into results, how approximately we begin via assessing your present function, it is the preliminary step to any hobby trade.

For instance, whenever I meet a candidate, the most crucial aspect I request is a finished account set of working duties:

"So, permit me understand, Bonnie," I begin, "What should it's which you do at your gift agency?"

"Well Dave, I idea I disclosed to you as of now. I'm a frameworks examiner."

"OK," I solution. "But ought to you please depict to me in detail the accompanying two matters:

1. What are your regular sports sports? That is, how may you spend a while all through a normal day?

2. What are the quantifiable results your business agency anticipates from the ones sports? At the save you of the day, how does your director understand at the same time as you are running surprisingly?" Frequently, I discover that people aren't able to do not forget reliable solutions about the precise concept of their art work. They're now not secure with their interest duties, and their absence of attention brings about strain or counter-productivity. Numerous businesses expect you recognize what they need and the manner that have to be completed, regularly without presenting you with grievance until after you have been ignored for that development you felt come to be merited. It is your hobby, and a part of being happy in it

for you and your manager is to be in agreement and meet or surpass goals and goals you each set.

While a tad of strain may also is normal in any hobby, a long-lasting ingesting everyday of it can demolish your motivation to art work and extensively impact bliss in all intervals of your existence. When you check your workweek joined at the side of your modern-day electricity, a top notch many people paintings extra than the relaxation (or do something else), so limiting any worry in your lifestyles affords to lifestyles's delight. An ongoing document affirms this and shows an immediate connection amongst an person's absence of challenge lucidity and their stage of employee dissatisfaction. Recognizing what you need is the pivotal initial step forgetting what's most proper for you. Each good buy you're making undermines your intention of vocational satisfaction and personal accomplishment. Requesting what you want demonstrates, you are targeted, keen, and assured approximately your aptitudes, aspirations, and capacities. Proactively shifting closer to your paintings along those strains will as a favored rule intrigue the humans you need to (if they may be the proper human beings), and could make prepared to you locating satisfaction and an high-quality in shape inside the workplace.

Attempt this hobby:

On a sheet of paper, compose a whole, cutting-edge-day-day set of working obligations in that you listing your each day sports sports and their elegant, quantifiable results. This hobby may not simply enable you to make clear your view of your art work; it'll probably be beneficial in a while when you start to bring together a resume and impart to others exactly what you have done and what you're trying to find.

When you have got depicted each one of the components of your hobby, the subsequent diploma is to recognize the relationship among what you do and how you sense. I use the time period 'values' as a descriptor of private wishes, as a measuring maintain on with assist you:

Understand what types of paintings-related sports you truely apprehend;

Determine which goals or achievements are vital to you and provide you with a sense of pleasure; and

Evaluate whether or not or no longer your personal goals are in parity or amicability along with your hobby condition — a modern role.

Even even though it's honestly comfortable to disentangle which regular undertakings you genuinely appreciate, the challenge of investigating your private dreams may be precarious. That is due to the fact there are regular factors random on your hobby that might end up likely the maximum essential detail.

To show off this significance of characteristics in our critical leadership way, undergo in thoughts the accompanying:

Work searcher can flip down a position because of the fact he modified right right into a newbie competitor and he did no longer address the air tremendous wherein my client organisation modified into decided.

A candidate who become an prolonged separation sprinter. He took a function to a wonderful quantity due to the reality his new manager become furthermore a sprinter, and would understand his need to take off artwork two times each 365 days to run the New York City and Boston prolonged-distance races.

A professional that took a vocation with an corporation organisation that furnished him a downgrade, given that being profoundly crucial internal his modern boss' area of knowledge made him experience awkward.

The state of affairs proper here is, we as a whole have profoundly personal motivations which guide our expert options. It is critical to set up and make the ones acknowledged.

Since you understand a way to represent your developments, the following degree is to depict the changes you would like to make in your new feature. To similarly illustrate, music in to the manner Pat, Craig, and Neil communicate approximately their precise times, and how they think about their traits:

Pat:

"I need to have greater self-sufficiency in which I artwork. That would likely mean having an adaptable calendar, operating distinct hours every day at my warning, without asking consent. I'd almost in reality leave proper off the bat Thursdays to take my girl to her appearing elegance, and consequently, I'd be satisfied to spend a few hours working at home inside the route of the night time and on ends of the week. With my private laptop, I'd technique my modem to the database in my vicinity of information, and I'd almost in fact make a notable willpower to the workload, whenever, day or night time. Most importantly, I'd be assessed absolutely on my exhibition, no longer thru the type of hours I've checked in."

Craig:

"I'd want to paintings nearer to my home. I failed to assume the degree of time I spent using have become essential once I joined the organisation years again, however now it really wears on me to sit down for an hour every day in rush hour gridlock. It's not truely nerve- wracking to control all of the insane human beings on the road; I may be the usage of the driving time to be with my circle of relatives. The lower in stress could improve my frame of thoughts and offer me higher private delight. If I should discover a vocation like what I encompass now inner a couple of minutes of home, that might make me glad."

Neil:

"I'm keen on my expert achievement. If I stay at this organisation an extra of longer, I will ought to art work on my own right into a nook in fact and in no manner accomplish my functionality.

Somebody, as of overdue requested me whether or now not I helped humans get "higher" occupations or employments that made them greater comfortable. My answer changed into that the 2 had been one within the equal. As any backer of aim putting will permit you to recognise, the more precisely you are organized to impart what you are seeking out, the faster and all the greater efficiently you will have the selection to get what you need.

Another attention is, in case you were to take a gander at your career from an important perspective, I should come up with four effective reasons why it makes experience to trade occupations within the equivalent or comparable company 3 instances in the course of your preliminary ten years of employer:

1.Changing occupations gives you a extra big base of records:

After round 3 years, you've got tailored the greater excellent a part of what you will keep in mind a manner to carry out your obligation. In this way, over a multi-12 months period, you purchased involvement from "three instances 90 percent" than "one-time 100 percentage."

2.A frequently fluctuated foundation makes a extra noteworthy interest on your talents:

The profundity of experience method you are increasingly more huge to a bigger variety of managers. You're no longer simply acquainted collectively with your present day-day business company's product, manipulate, strategies, great duties, inventory framework, and so forth.; you deliver with you the know-how you have picked up out of your previous paintings with particular corporations.

three.-Workchangebringsabout a quickened development cycle:

With a distinction you may leap, for instance, from challenge fashion designer to senior mission architect; or countrywide institution consequences in VP of gives and showcasing.

4.More obligation activates extra wonderful acquiring electricity:

A reimbursement increment normally joins improvement. What's more, because you're advanced quicker, your pay develops at a snappier pace, much like exacerbating the pinnacle class you'll procure on a certificate of the store.

While there is no preventing the crucial thing excellencies from claiming particular employment changing with the surrender goal of vocation have an impact on, you want to make sure the manner you are taking will lead you wherein you virtually want to go. There is subsequently little motivation to make a vocation change for more cash if the subsequent frustrations make you depressed to the element of distraction. Not very an extended manner in the past, I set a undertaking engineer with an organization that extended to him a $forty seven,000 a yr art work. He later confided to me that that day he consented to get all the manner right down to corporation for my purchaser, he'd grew to become down an idea of $83, hundred with the opponent company. The purpose? The better provide was a counseling role with an aviation commercial enterprise enterprise in Detroit - artwork that would have delivered him down a road he felt modified proper right into a pause.

The "first rate" work is one wherein your features are being commonly fulfilled accurately. If vocation improvement and headway are your essential goals, and they've spoken to through way of the quantity you got, at that thing, the hobby that can pay the maximum coins is regularly the "better" art work. Your obligation while considering a trade is to evaluate what is most crucial to you. Regardless of whether or not you attention on a single part of your interest (like Craig, Neil and Pat did), or on the overall idea of the commercial enterprise you want to beautify, the extra manifestly you interface your tendencies along with your paintings, the more prominent the capability for employee pride.

How You Can Be Happier In Life

Where attention goes, electricity streams.You may also have heard this articulation, or a few edition of it, for your actions. What we middle round, grows - and this modern day may be linked supportively whether or not or no longer we want to decrease the concern in a particular a part of our lives or we need to improve our intimate connections.

Easier stated than executed? Maybe. It is one thing to concur with this concept or see the notion in this rationally. It is a few component else out and out to get it- - to revel in an "a-ha" minute in which this turns out to be clean and valid for YOU, no longer because of the truth any person permit you to understand so.

This actual understanding originates from a lived know-how of the fact - the results - of the concept. Also, a huge detail humans desires the lived expertise over and over till we "get" it. In a minute, I will impart to you a tool that, after a while, can help provide you with a felt-experience or more profound comprehension of the intensity of this idea.

Right off the bat, but, I'd want to assertion on the manner that during our western culture we're quite adapted to guide with our minds, and alongside the ones lines, we can, in preferred, be given a massive portion of what we assume.

A considerable lot dad and mom within the west are however in kindergarten in terms of an knowledge of the whole idea of the mind. Therefore, whilst we revel in terrible musings about a person or problem earlier than we comprehend it, we are able to find out ourselves marinating in that adverse or critical united states of america. Also, both without delay or after a time, this state affects our emotional and bodily reality.

How may want to we free ourselves from this spot in which we're, at very last, caught via our very non-public minds?

Straightforward sluggish steps will take us to a extra profound comprehension of what our minds are designed to do and the manner we do ourselves an insult at the identical time as we placed the thoughts in the purpose pressure's seat without, well, putting off to driving force's schooling.

So- - how approximately we get possible about a manner to artwork with this notion.

The initial step to liberating ourselves from the snare we once in a while create with our minds is excessively critical: we need to end up privy to the concept of our reasoning.

Indeed, even critical mindfulness can deliver us the gap to be absolutely a superb deal tons less diagnosed with something idea/s we trust at that point. If we do not know, and we are used to the sentiment of being in a horrible u

. S . Or perhaps numb, we might not make the following stride.

How would probable we come to be aware?

Typically the number one sign that we are accepting awful issues is from the emotional existence wherein we feel a clumsy feeling, as an instance, dread, outrage, or sorrow, or now and again the piece of statistics is from the body on the identical time as we suppose weariness, torment, progressing ailment, or considered one of a type aspect results.

In this manner, if you see any of those emotions or side consequences, stop and start to appearance what and the manner you're wondering proper then and there.

When you have got grew to end up out to endure in mind of your horrible deduction at that time, you are prepared for the following degree.

A part of the extra beneficial belongings for the following degree (which I use with my customers) are beyond the volume of a ebook. However, I will depart you with the concept that is easy and may be beneficial to break out of contrary reasoning.

Martin Seligman, one of the organizers of Positive Psychology, and the writer of the books Learned Optimism, and Authentic Happiness says that as indicated with the aid of his examination, a self-assured person and a worrywart variety in an important, important manner as a protracted manner as how they view destructive and effective activities.

Are you recreation? Here's the juice:

Basically, a confident man or woman considers opposite to be in life as quick and precise to that scenario or episode, (for instance, "I didn't do well on that check due to the reality I wasn't feeling admirable that day") and super things as changeless and all-inclusive, (for example, "I had been given superior due to the fact I'm proper at my unique employment.)

On the opportunity hand, a worrier does the inverse: makes impermanent and unique clarifications for development, (as an instance, "I actually have emerge as in truth fortunate"), and perpetual and elegant descriptions for mishaps, (as an example, "Nobody ever will pay hobby to my mind.")

Why is this critical?

Here's the critical end result to this distinction in deduction: inquire about demonstrates that self-assured human beings pass once more from issues energetically and jump on a roll efficaciously when they prevail as fast as, at the same time as doubters allow misfortunes in a unmarried trouble in their lives have an effect on the various factors in their lives, more frequently than no longer for quite a while period, and every so often jump on a roll.

Figuring out a way to be a hopeful man or woman is vital in your existence!

Medicine for Happiness:

In this way, to be extra pleased in a relationship, or with the instances of life, proper right here's the fundamental, however now not easy, -phase remedy:

1.When life indicates a time or someone accomplishes some issue that upsets you, make a splendid try to find a convincing impermanent and particular reason of it (as an instance "She modified into tired," "he grow to be feeling horrible," "I didn't sense well that day" as opposed to "she in no manner tunes in to meâ," he is this type of malcontent," or "I can not perform a little issue right.")

2.When any man or woman (as an instance your lifestyles accomplice, relative, leader) accomplishes something terrific, beautify it in your mind with credible clarifications which is probably lasting (usually) and inescapable (related to character tendencies.) Forinstance, "she's so keen," or "I continuously bypass for what I want" in preference to "they provided her a reprieve" or "I'm truly lucky."

I want to underline that is really now not a way to stay willfully ignorant or live in a harsh state of affairs. If you're in an emotionally or bodily traumatic state of affairs, get a few issue assist you need to get out.

This is additionally no longer a choice to push aside the concerned or furious portions of ourselves; if you find out that the ones views are often in control, this is the location art work with an representative may be useful, to really assist you to get to the foundation of the other reasoning.

But, in case you are upset with a few part of your life, your mate, or your courting, and also you in truth change your thoughts, watch and phrase, because of the truth the world may also begin to change itself straight away in advance than you!

Chapter 5: Why Should I Change And Where Do I Start?

Reason

One primary motive is the craving to exchange topics because of the reality you are not exactly enthusiastic about how subjects are. You may probably want to trade or beautify your properly being and well-being, your public hobby, your vocation or business enterprise, your cash related situation, or discover your very non-public significance in lifestyles.

Another valid justification may be to show into your high-quality self (immoderate highbrow self-portrait and vanity) and shape life situations to shape a advanced future. Have the choice to govern problems excellently, be answerable for making your very personal existence, and form your call into claim emblem of one. As a rule, the profound placed reason for non-public troubles is sub-par mental self-view.

Possibly you are searching out statistics and comprehension of self, humanity, the area, and the Universe. That is to consciously expand and recognize the enjoy of your gift existence experience. At that issue later deliver once more your competencies and recognise-how to the sector.

So do no longer in reality act in reality - be in reality the splendid, and expect duty in your existence. Purposefully choose what you want and work on attaining it. Structure of your destiny attempts not to provide all people a threat to shape conditions of your tomorrow.

Become greater, so that you can do more, with the reason that you could Have more.

hard to recognize

The people who take a seat within the hover of their introduction are folks who're tranquil and satisfied.

obscure

Profound somewhere inside the massive majority human beings need big serenity and bliss - or in different phrases, we need to stay in a circumstance of affection:to adore how we stay to adore how we enjoy to like doing what we love to be cherished, esteemed and regarded through others to be lovely, profitable and aware to specific humans to percentage our pride with the humans we love to affectionately make contributions our incentive to humankind

Inspiration

First, you want to triumph over the thoughts/body obstruction and showcase that you in truth need the alternate. From individual revel in, I understand that it's miles difficult to behavior, beliefs or trade food regimen. In any case, while you show that you propose it, you can get awesome help from the inner truely as from absolutely everyone round you.

Also, each one of the blessings (being lean, feeling strength, feeling efficient, and so on) will persuade you to maintain onward. The entire change appears to be easy and a chunk of the upgraded you. By then it is hard lending to go back to the antique approaches.

Accomplishing a one hundred% final results includes of ninety nine% profound motive and precise interest and genuinely 1% method - you could always discover away.

difficult to recognize

Each system begins offevolved with 1 degree, one partner, 1 pound, 1 greenback - tolerance and staying strength gets you wherein you want to be. If you are at the economic limit or have a short length to your day, it is nonetheless in reality feasible, and it will actually take a chunk longer.

The first rate technique to start is to stop speaking and begin doing.

The international is evolving. I am tremendous you've got were given heard it a few place or professional it yourself. Presently is the opportune time to make modifications to development effects into the today's period of Generation WE. It's not very past due. You can do it!

Concentrate on one intention right away, ideally one an amazing manner to mission and push you. Get acquainted with the hypothesis, go out and exercising, harm down discoveries and beautify. Give the development a risk to be your idea. Continue onward and hold at it. Sooner or later subjects will start to get much less complex.

"Effective people percent one component in like manner: staying electricity at perceiving what satisfies them. This is the detail that makes you precise. This is your distinctiveness better than ninety nine% of human beings reachable. This is the area your boundless abundance of gaining knowledge of and euphoria dwells. It typically involves you; you are pressured to do it. You need to bear in mind it, live it, and make a residing using it."

Be placing, have a ton of a laugh, go out on a limb, make a change, depart an inheritance. Try no longer to pass up the enjoy of lifestyles. You are a unique and incredible man or woman, pre-forced out at some stage in childbirth with a very unique functionality this is specifically profitable to humankind.

Quite some time from now you may be regularly disillusioned thru the property you did now not do than via those you probably did. So, free the start. Go a ways from the protected harbor. Catch the change winds your sails. Investigate. Dream. Find.

Get Your Work done

You want to do a piece of schoolwork to maintain your self on direction and stimulated and to be increasingly more sensitive to situations and bizarre synchronicities on the way to arise round you.

Consider things you as of now love approximately yourself and your life. Consider real parts of your lifestyles and be grateful that you as of now have a extraordinary head start! Appreciation is the concept of each beneficial aspect. Watch The Secret a few times and supply unusual attention to the thoughts of appreciation, outlook, and growing a circulate.

Next, don't forget your Resources you as of now have. That implies basics, for instance, nourishment and haven (no matter whether or not it technique living at the side of your mother and father), pay or keep in mind of a Visa enterprise, your pals who adore you and bolster you (regardless of whether or not or no longer or not it's far simply 1 of them), and your contacts that could open entryways for you (another time, no matter whether it's best 1 character).

At that factor, keep in mind your gold standard lifestyles. If cash, time, or information changed into no item, what sort of existence ought to probable you want to have:

Who may you want to be?

What might you need to do?

Where might also moreover you need to stay?

What home may additionally additionally you need to have?

What apparatuses or matters could in all likelihood you need to have?

What form of friends or pal may want to you want?

What form of own family life might probably you want to have?

You need to be as unique as you may be: the accurate image of your self, particular spots, cautious gadgets, specific communications, spiritual feelings. Record this.

Whatever the psyche can do not forget and get maintain of, the brain can accomplish.

Request Feedback

If you've got were given reliable and honest buddies or family, you may ask them straight away to depict you (as an instance give you three modifiers about you) or to expose to you in which you want to decorate. Try no longer to contend, do now not declaration, do no longer utter a word besides a solitary "Much obliged."

I remember it's miles nice in case you ask them via e-mail, so as that they've the possibility to preserve in thoughts. You can likewise encompass a bit disclaimer that you're seeking out splendid feedback and some component they will be of splendid incentive to you as you took a shot at non-public development. Tailor the phrases to the form of courting you've got were given with them.

Think and contemplate their answers. Take as a extraordinary deal time as is wanted, even an afternoon or . This is the manner others see you. If you do now not deal with it, you want to trade the way you present your self to mirror the "right" you.

Remember that the work to alternate the out of doors starts offevolved with the paintings on the inner that is conduct, reactions, disposition, and conduct. Legitimately disclosing to them how they will be incorrect might not function. You need to truly and reliably run over how you need via your everyday activities.

If you arrive at the resolution that they'll be onto some thing, you want to decide to decorate proper here. It should be YOUR CONSCIOUS DECISION to enhance for the machine to paintings.

New beginning

First, you need to smooth up the hooked up order to make location for the today's getting to know and behavior. Start with herbal cleaning: house, car, place of work, PC, body, and health. It is crucial to tidy this up as agonizing over the chaos will meddle on the same time as you're doing thoughts, coronary coronary heart, and soul cleaning.

After physical cleaning, you may proceed onward to social condition, profound, excessive task subjects, improving substandard zones, and developing new conduct as a manner to assist you to be your exceptional.

Here's an incomplete rundown of a respectable start:

have an arrangement, preserve every day/month to month/every 12 months plan for the day, be powerful every day, hold focused hold the inspirational element of view, exercising session, make investments electricity in nature, meet with pals a piece

encircle your self with optimistic people, abstain from stepping into contentions with pessimistic humans

kind out your price range (manage, spending plan, integrate, mechanize installments)

Go out on a limb a, accept as true with that the subsequent diploma will seem to you as you are organized to take it. Inside half a month or months, you can wind up without a doubt excited for being on the new way. The way in which your frame, brain, coronary coronary heart, and soul is pleased and fulfilled.

If you lack time, you may soar without delay to what you experience you want to do. As you could come, the fashionable following degree will seem to you glaringly. You will find out in reality the ones recommendations beneficial, that you are organized to pay interest right now. Now after which you need to cross decrease returned to particular sports activities sports multiple months after the truth to see it from a splendid component and discover new understanding.

You have to apprehend in which you are going. The appropriate responses will come to you voluntarily.

Supplant Limiting Beliefs

I started out with fixing all my restricting convictions and getting a sturdy established order to extend on; To exchange a existence, you have to break modern limiting examples and circles:

Discernment + Behavior + Structure => Change personal pride

If your behavior and beliefs did now not get you the lifestyles you want so far, you want to move outside of your international and test. You can't repair or decorate what you do not suppose even about. One exceptional method to get spherical this problem (in case you dare) is to country to your self (and suggest it) this assertion:

I plan to be examined the top of my limiting belief, and what lies past them.

Inside days or a day, you may begin to encounter conditions in that you every take a look at a few element one in every of a type to you, or without problem enjoy some trouble that you recently notion have become outlandish or difficult, or you'll be located instantaneous and want to manipulate some difficulties.

The huge concept here is to supplant the Limiting Beliefs with Empowering ones. If to date you aren't very glad with how your life is going, it seems which you want to alternate the way you hold in thoughts or do positive subjects (short and long term). This hobby is meant to acquaint you with new picks and new intuition to take in addition actions and grow to be with new effects.

Madness: doing likewise time and again and searching forward to excellent results.

Addition the Knowledge

Making the notable of ourselves is the purpose we were conceived, however it requires staying electricity and balance. The time has come to understand your imaginative and prescient of your high-quality self - and your most extended amount of self belief. You have the right to come upon intense fearlessness and dignity, and to bear in mind your self to be the character you want to be.

Choose what you want to improve on your lifestyles. Is it well being, nicely being, appearance, education, viability, self notion, vocation, commercial commercial enterprise organisation, social talents, connections, or the manner to provide lower back to humanity? In a notable worldwide, that is some element you are obsessed on. Keep in mind that it want to be YOUR obsession, no longer any person else's.

Pick your teach who is an ace at the ability you need to investigate and with whom you experience appropriate. You don't need to recognize that person for my part, so long as there can be a way you may become acquainted with the lessons. The absolutely crucial and vital initial step is to make a aware desire which you really want to make the change. The next improvement is to research, apply, and exercising.

Pick a studying technique that is extremely good for you (perusing books, searching recordings, tuning in to internet recordings, looking through the internet, studying with the resource of doing, or the majority of the abovementioned). At that difficulty, pick out out what precisely you need to advantage and the amount you need to study (1/2, 80%, 90%, or 100% and grow to be an ace your self). Recall the product programming 90-90 guiding principle, which applies to test almost some thing new in existence:

It requires a few investment to do ninety%, and every other 90% to do the final 10%.

If you do now not understand the quantity you need to are trying to find after the authority, start, and you will discover fast sufficient. For my state of affairs, I went for round 70-eighty five% authority of elegant skills. Necessarily appropriate sufficient and in some time, I proceeded onward to the subsequent expert. At times in which I certainly extremely happy inside the potential, I went for eighty 5-a hundred%.

Strong self-restraint and taught staying electricity are critical to the excessive lifestyles.

Keep in thoughts that no degree of perusing will set you up for the genuine e-book like this. It is critical to understand the requirements and tips, however, ultimately you need to jump on that bull night time time membership, tennis court docket, some issue. Start little from the outset, make little one strides, and preserve pushing earlier. Be quiet. Do the whole thing determinedly and truly. Watch your reality converting before your eyes.

Chapter 6: Understanding The Importance Of Saying "No"

Learning to mention "no" is not easy, but it is an crucial capacity for creating healthful barriers and retaining your highbrow fitness and well-being. Saying "certain" to the whole lot can cause exhaustion, burnout, or perhaps resentment towards others. In this economic smash, we're capable of find out the benefits of putting obstacles, the outcomes of constantly pronouncing "advantageous," and the impact of announcing "no" to your intellectual fitness and properly-being.

The Benefits of Setting Boundaries:

Setting boundaries is an crucial part of developing a healthful and enjoyable lifestyles. Boundaries assist us to outline what's and isn't always appropriate in our relationships and interactions with others. Some of the blessings of placing limitations encompass:

Improving your intellectual and emotional fitness: Setting boundaries can assist lessen pressure and anxiety, in addition to save you burnout and exhaustion. When you positioned limitations, you create region to prioritize your very very own dreams and properly-being, that could enhance your widespread intellectual and emotional fitness.

Strengthening your relationships: Healthy obstacles can make more potent relationships through growing accept as true with and appreciate among people. When you talk your dreams and obstacles in reality, others are more likely to understand and admire your perspective.

Boosting your vanity: Setting boundaries and announcing "no" whilst important can raise your conceitedness with the resource of speaking that your desires and emotions are valid and crucial.

The Consequences of Constantly Saying "Yes":

While it could appear to be announcing "sure" to the whole lot is the top notch way to pride others and avoid conflict, constantly pronouncing "positive" must have terrible consequences, collectively with:

Burnout and exhaustion: Constantly announcing "certain" to others can cause feeling overwhelmed and overcommitted, ensuing in burnout and exhaustion.

Resentment inside the path of others: When you prioritize others' goals over your very personal constantly, it could purpose resentment and frustration toward others, despite the fact that they're not intentionally causing damage.

Decreased productivity and overall performance: When you're overcommitted, it may be difficult to carry out at your wonderful, essential to decreased productiveness and typical overall performance.

The Impact of Saying "No" on Your Mental Health and Well-being:

Saying "no" may be tough, specifically if you are concerned approximately disappointing others or being seen as selfish. However, mastering to say "no" at the same time as crucial may have a nice effect to your mental fitness and nicely-being. Some of the advantages of saying "no" embody:

Reducing strain and tension: Saying "no" can assist lessen stress and tension via allowing you to prioritize your very very very own wishes and well-being.

Promoting self-care: Saying "no" allows you to prioritize self-care and make an effort to relaxation and recharge.

Increasing self-admire: When you are saying "no," you're speaking that your dreams and feelings are valid and essential, that might increase yourself-admire and arrogance.

In end, setting obstacles and analyzing to say "no" is an critical a part of keeping your highbrow health and properly-being. While it is able to be tough to mention "no" in the beginning, the benefits of prioritizing your non-public desires and well-being are properly well worth it. In the subsequent chapters, we can find out techniques and techniques for saying "no" with a bit of luck and assertively.

Chapter 7: Identifying Your Needs And Priorities

In order to find out how to say "no" optimistically and assertively, it's far crucial to first recognize your needs and priorities. This financial catastrophe will find out a manner to discover your desires and priorities, the significance of self-awareness and self-care, and the impact of neglecting your private wishes.

How to Identify Your Needs and Priorities:

Identifying your goals and priorities entails taking the time to mirror on what's critical to you and what you need to prioritize to your life. Some useful techniques to apprehend your goals and priorities encompass:

Journaling: Writing down your thoughts and emotions allow you to advantage readability and discover what's critical to you.

Reflecting on beyond reports: Reflecting on past research in which you felt fulfilled and glad will will permit you to discover what brings you satisfaction and fulfillment.

Asking for remarks: Asking for feedback from trusted pals or circle of relatives human beings can offer perception into your strengths and values.

The Importance of Self-Awareness and Self-Care:

Self-cognizance and self-care are crucial for figuring out your needs and priorities. Self-awareness includes statistics your thoughts, feelings, and behaviors, even as self-care consists of searching after your physical, intellectual, and emotional properly-being. When you prioritize self-interest and self-care, you're better capable of pick out out your goals and set boundaries that honor your values and priorities.

The Impact of Neglecting Your Own Needs:

Neglecting your very private desires may additionally moreover have a bad effect to your mental and physical fitness, in addition to your relationships with others. When you neglect about approximately your personal needs, you could feel green with envy or crushed, crucial to expanded strain and tension. Additionally, neglecting your very non-public goals can cause reduced productivity and well-known performance, similarly to strained relationships with others.

In cease, identifying your dreams and priorities is an crucial a part of learning to mention "no" with a chunk of success and assertively. When you prioritize self-recognition and self-care, you are better capable of perceive your goals and set limitations that honor your values and priorities. In the following chapters, we are capable of discover techniques for putting boundaries and pronouncing "no" with a bit of success and assertively.

Chapter 8: Overcoming The Fear Of Saying "No"

Saying "no" can be tough, specifically whilst we fear disappointing others or worry the outcomes of turning down a request. In this economic catastrophe, we are able to find out commonplace fears and anxieties round announcing "no," techniques for overcoming fear and building self notion, and the strength of assertiveness and standing up for yourself.

Common Fears and Anxieties Around Saying "No":

Some not unusual fears and anxieties spherical saying "no" include:

Fear of rejection or disapproval: We may additionally worry that pronouncing "no" will bring about others rejecting us or disapproving people.

Fear of lacking out: We may also worry that saying "no" will result in missing out on opportunities or reviews.

Fear of war: We may also moreover worry that pronouncing "no" will bring about conflict or tension in our relationships.

Techniques for Overcoming Fear and Building Confidence:

There are numerous techniques that could help us conquer our fears and assemble self notion in announcing "no":

Practice saying "no": Start small with the aid of the usage of announcing "no" to small requests or conditions that enjoy solid. This allow you to assemble self assure for your capacity to set limitations.

Reframe your mind-set: Instead of seeing pronouncing "no" as a negative or egocentric act, reframe it as a exceptional motion this is crucial in your properly-being.

Use assertive communique: Assertive communication consists of expressing your desires and goals in a clean and respectful manner. This will let you enjoy greater assured in announcing "no" and status up for yourself.

The Power of Assertiveness and Standing Up for Yourself:

Assertiveness is a treasured capability for placing boundaries and standing up for yourself. When we are assertive, we are capable of explicit our needs and goals in a easy and respectful manner, at the same time as additionally respecting the dreams and goals of others. Assertiveness can assist us construct stronger relationships, decorate our communication abilities, and increase our vanity.

In stop, overcoming the concern of saying "no" is an vital step in setting barriers and prioritizing our desires. By figuring out our fears and anxieties, the use of strategies to conquer them, and running within the path of assertive conversation, we are able to construct self belief in our functionality to say "no" and get up for ourselves.

Chapter 9: Saying "No" With Confidence

Now that we have explored the importance of announcing "no," identified our dreams and priorities, and triumph over our fears and anxieties, it's time to analyze the way to say "no" with self notion. In this financial disaster, we will communicate techniques for saying "no" assertively and hopefully, how to speak your desires correctly, and strategies for dealing with pushback and hard conversations.

Techniques for Saying "No" Assertively and Confidently:

Use "I" statements: Start your reaction with "I" statements that assert your wishes and emotions. For instance, "I'm sorry, but I can't determine to that proper now."

Be clean and direct: Don't beat at some stage in the bush or make excuses. Say "no" straight away and in reality, but also respectfully.

Use a enterprise but polite tone: You can say "no" civilly and however be assertive. Speak with a corporation however polite tone to carry your message.

How to Communicate Your Needs Effectively:

Know your limits: Be privy to your limits and obstacles, and communicate them definitely to others.

Practice lively listening: Active listening includes listening to the other character's desires and issues and responding in a manner that shows you recognize their mind-set.

Use "I" statements: Use "I" statements to particular your very very own goals and emotions, and keep away from blaming or criticizing others.

Strategies for Handling Pushback and Difficult Conversations:

Be respectful: Respect the opposite man or woman's perspective and feelings, even if you don't remember them.

Stay calm: Stay calm and composed, despite the fact that the alternative individual becomes defensive or aggressive.

Be open to compromise: Consider compromising with the alternative character if it is feasible to discover a answer that meets every of your dreams.

In give up, saying "no" with self perception includes the use of assertive verbal exchange, know-how your limits and boundaries, and managing pushback and hard conversations with apprehend and composure. By schooling those strategies and techniques, you can communicate your wishes correctly and prioritize your very very own properly-being.

Chapter 10: Navigating Guilt And Disappointing Others

In previous chapters, we've got got discussed the importance of pronouncing "no" and strategies for doing so with a piece of success and effectively. However, for plenty people, the act of saying "no" can be followed via way of manner of feelings of guilt and the fear of disappointing others. In this financial disaster, we will explore the placement of guilt in pronouncing "no," techniques for managing guilt, and the way to deal with disappointing others at the same time as prioritizing your very own needs.

Understanding the Role of Guilt in Saying "No":

Guilt is a commonplace emotion related to saying "no" to others. It can stem from a revel in of duty to pleasure others, fear of rejection, or a desire to keep away from conflict. However, allowing guilt to manual your desire-making can purpose resentment, burnout, and an incapacity to prioritize your personal goals.

Strategies for Managing Guilt and Finding Peace with Your Decisions:

Recognize your feelings: Acknowledge and take delivery of your feelings of guilt without judgment. Recognize that it is ordinary to feel this manner, but it might no longer suggest you need to compromise your very private properly-being.

Challenge your thoughts: Question your ideals and mind that may be contributing in your emotions of guilt. Ask your self, "Is this perception beneficial?" or "Is this perception based totally on reality?"

Practice self-compassion: Treat your self with the identical kindness and understanding you would provide to a friend. Be mild with your self and allow yourself to make errors.

How to Handle Disappointing Others While Prioritizing Your Needs:

Be sincere: Be sincere and transparent with others approximately your motives for announcing "no." Communicate your desires surely and respectfully.

Offer alternatives: If feasible, offer alternative solutions or suggestions that could meet every of your dreams.

Set limitations: Set clean obstacles with others and stick with them. Be assertive in communicating your obstacles, and do not permit others stress you into compromising them.

In end, handling feelings of guilt and managing disappointing others on the equal time as prioritizing your non-public goals is an important detail of reading to mention "no." By spotting and difficult your thoughts, working toward self-compassion, and setting obstacles, you could make selections that align collectively together along with your values and properly-being, while nonetheless retaining healthy relationships with others.

Chapter 11: Setting Boundaries And Maintaining Them

In the preceding chapters, we cited the importance of setting boundaries and pronouncing "no" to prioritize your goals. In this bankruptcy, we can delve deeper into the way to set healthful barriers with others, the importance of consistency and observe-via, and hints for keeping limitations to save you burnout.

How to Set Healthy Boundaries with Others:

Identify your goals: Know what you need to sense secure, first rate, and fulfilled for your relationships.

Be easy: Communicate your barriers definitely and assertively to others. Let them comprehend what conduct is not suitable to you and what you count on from them.

Start small: Set small limitations and frequently constructing up to extra sizeable ones. This technique can help you bring together self guarantee in putting and maintaining obstacles.

The Importance of Consistency and Follow-via:

Be steady: Once you placed a boundary, hold on with it. Consistency is fundamental to keeping healthful boundaries and constructing take delivery of as actual with with others.

Follow-via: If a person crosses your boundary, have a look at via with the effects you've got have been given set up. This reinforces the importance of your limitations and lets in others understand that they need to recognize them.

Tips for Maintaining Boundaries and Preventing Burnout:

Take care of yourself: Self-care is important for preserving wholesome limitations and stopping burnout. Take breaks, engage in sports sports that make you revel in proper, and exercise self-compassion.

Practice announcing "no": Saying "no" can be tough, however it is a vital potential for setting and keeping boundaries. Practice announcing "no" mainly situations to bring together self assurance and red meat up your boundaries.

Seek guide: Surround your self with folks who respect your boundaries and provide assist even as you need it. Having a supportive community allow you to keep wholesome limitations and prevent burnout.

In quit, setting wholesome boundaries with others is crucial for keeping healthy relationships and preventing burnout. By identifying your desires, being clear and constant together together with your limitations, and schooling self-care, you may create a supportive and enjoyable life for yourself.

Chapter 12: The Power Of Saying "Yes" To Yourself

In the preceding chapters, we've discussed the significance of putting boundaries, saying "no," and prioritizing your desires. In this financial ruin, we are capable of explore the energy of announcing "certain" to your self, the benefits of prioritizing your wishes and self-care, and suggestions for cultivating a wholesome dating with your self.

How Saying "No" Can Help You Say "Yes" to Yourself:

Saying "no" to others manner announcing "sure" to yourself: When you say "no" to others, you are saying "yes" to yourself and your dreams. This will let you prioritize self-care and create a satisfying life for your self.

Setting barriers can enhance your relationships: Setting barriers can improve your relationships with the resource of assisting you communicate your needs and create more healthy dynamics with others.

This can free up greater time and electricity an extraordinary manner to interest on yourself.

The Benefits of Prioritizing Your Needs and Self-Care:

Improved highbrow and bodily fitness: Prioritizing your dreams and tasty in self-care can decorate your highbrow and bodily health through the usage of reducing strain and developing fashionable nicely-being.

Increased conceitedness and self guarantee: Prioritizing your goals can increase your self-esteem and self assure through reinforcing your self-worth and validating your boundaries.

Tips for Cultivating a Healthy Relationship with Yourself:

Practice self-compassion: Treat yourself with kindness and information, just as you will address a near pal or cherished one.

Engage in self-care: Take time for your self every day to have interaction in sports that carry you pleasure, rest, and rejuvenation.

Set personal goals: Set desires for yourself that align together collectively with your values and passions. This will can help you cultivate a experience of motive and fulfillment.

In end, pronouncing "no" to others can be a effective tool for pronouncing "sure" to your self and prioritizing your wishes. By prioritizing self-care, enhancing your relationships thru boundary-placing, and cultivating a healthy courting with your self, you may create a fulfilling lifestyles that aligns along with your values and passions.

www.ingramcontent.com/pod-product-compliance
Lightning Source LLC
Chambersburg PA
CBHW061506050726
47593CB00002B/484